E
175.5   Winston
F545   John Fiske.

72-461

Date Due

JUL 2000

JUN 2004

JUL X X 2015

WITHDRAWN

Twayne's United States Authors Series

Sylvia E. Bowman, *Editor*

INDIANA UNIVERSITY

John Fiske

JOHN FISKE

By GEORGE P. WINSTON

Nichols College

 197

Twayne Publishers, Inc. :: New York

To My Mother and Father

Preface

At the beginning of the twentieth century, John Fiske was regarded by many as one of the American giants. After some years of neglect, his work is once again appearing in anthologies. Therefore, my major task has been to attempt an evaluation of this work to assess its value for us as the century draws to a close.

In looking back over my now rather long and intimate association with John Fiske through his works, I have come to the conclusion that his rightful place lies somewhat above midway between that which he held at his death and that which he has held since that time: certainly in placing his writings against the whole fabric of American culture, we cannot continue to argue that he is one of the handful of major figures; no more does he deserve to be one of America's forgotten men.

In adding one more to a rather large gallery of sketches and portraits, I have intended to focus my interpretation on two main points of evaluation. First, John Fiske as a Victorian. From his life and work we find vividly portrayed an illustration of the age: not a type nor even a representative, but a real, live Victorian. For moderns, a clearer understanding of the American Victorian is at least as essential as an understanding of any portion of our past. Too long have we been aware of the sharp break between us and unaware of the continuum. My second point has been to assay a few suggestions as to some of the concrete threads of the continuum displayed in the works of Fiske: what does he have to say to us today? If I have succeeded in performing this task, I have underscored the reasons why Fiske is still a figure of importance.

No critical study can or should say all that there is to say, but the author fondly hopes that his book will in one sense resemble an iceberg. Thus I hope I have by implication suggested Fiske as in some respects a Victorian synthesis of the classic Jonathan Edwards=Benjamin Franklin dichotomy in

American literature. Just as Fiske detected a bond of sympathy between the Puritan and the Darwinian scientist, so—facing about in time—I detect a bond between Fiske and relatively new areas like ecology and American studies. There are echoes of John Fiske, historian, in Samuel Eliot Morison's *Intellectual Life of Colonial New England* and Carl Becker's *Beginnings of the American People*; and the poet-scientist speaks again in Loren Eiseley's *The Immense Journey*.

My specific approach has been to separate the various strands of Fiske's career and treat these chronologically in turn. Since a major portion of the subject matter of his lectures appeared again in his books or articles, I have forborne to discuss these materials in the section on Fiske as lecturer; they can best be assessed, after the lapse of years, in their printed form.

No writer can hope to acknowledge all of the assistance he has received, directly and indirectly, from people and from reading, when he completes a task such as this. I should like, however, to extend my sincere thanks to Professor James R. Vitelli; Mrs. Donald Haines of the Petersham Historical Society; Mr. Robert G. Gennett of the Skillman Library, Lafayette College; and Miss Susan Flint, John Fiske's granddaughter.

GEORGE P. WINSTON

Nichols College

Contents

Chronology

1842   Edmund Fisk Green, only son of Edmund Brewster Green and Mary Fisk Bound Green, born March 30 in Middletown, Connecticut.

1852   Edmund Green, Sr., dies of cholera in Panama.

1855   March, Mary Green marries Edwin Wallace Stoughton. May, young Edmund enters Betts Academy, Stamford, Connecticut. September, legally changes his name to John Fisk, at his grandmother's request. (The "e" was added in 1860.)

1857   John is graduated from Betts Academy. Begins study with the Reverend Colton.

1859   Takes and passes entrance examinations for Yale; requests to be allowed to go to Harvard instead.

1860   Problems with orthodox religion. May, leaves for Cambridge to complete studies for Harvard. August, passes Harvard entrance examinations with sophomore standing. September, visits Ralph Waldo Emerson in Concord.

1861   October, receives "public admonition" and is nearly suspended from college for reading in church. December, publishes his first article, a critical commentary on Henry Thomas Buckle, in the *National Quarterly Review*.

1862   Engaged to Abby Morgan Brooks of Petersham, Massachusetts.

1863   Is graduated from Harvard; serves as class poet. October, publishes second article, "The Evolution of Language," *North American Review*. Enters Harvard Law School.

1864   July, admitted to the Boston bar. September 6, marries Abby Morgan Brooks. Attempts to practice law and carry on literary work as avocation.

1865   July 21, birth of first child, Maud.

1866   In the spring, gives up law; retires with his family to Middletown to marshal forces for a new career.

1867   March, returns to Cambridge, hopeful for the "new era" at Harvard. April, article on "University Reform" in the *Atlantic Monthly*. May 13, birth of first son, Harold Brooks.

1869   May 10, birth of another son, Clarence Stoughton. October, begins series of lectures as special lecturer at Harvard. Publication of *Tobacco and Alcohol*.

1870   Renominated lecturer at Harvard. Appointed acting professor of history. November 16, birth of fourth child, Ralph Browning.

1872   Begins lecture touring. Refused invitation to Lowell Institute. May, receives one-year appointment as assistant librarian at Harvard. *The Classroom Taine.* July 27, birth of second daughter, Ethel.

1873   *Myths and Mythmakers.* Mrs. M. A. Edwards donates money for European trip. Leave of absence granted, and library position made permanent. August 12, John sails for Europe with plans to convert lectures into a book.

1874   May, sails for home after grand tour and working and socializing with notables. *Outlines of Cosmic Philosophy.*

1876   *The Unseen World and Other Essays.*

1877   August 10, birth of sixth and last child, Herbert Huxley.

1878   Various factors turn Fiske's attention to American history.

1879   February, resigns position in Harvard library. March, course of six lectures at Old South Church on "America's Place in History." May, sails again for England and in June delivers lectures in London. June, elected to the Harvard Board of Overseers. October, opens new lecture series in Maine. *Darwinism and Other Essays. The Presidents of America.*

1880   Lectures in Philadelphia, Washington, Buffalo. May, third voyage to England, this time with Abby. Lectures at Royal Institution and in Edinburgh.

1881   Completes third lecture season in the United States. Agreement with Harpers to write *A Short History of the American People.*

1882   Mr. Stoughton dies. Mrs. Stoughton settles in Cambridge.

1883   January, sails for fourth and last time for England; illness forces return in April.

1884   Lectures at Bronson Alcott's Concord School. *The Destiny of Man. Excursions of an Evolutionist.*

1885   Second Concord lecture. *The Idea of God. American Political Ideas.* Assistant editor for Appleton's.

1886   Attempts lectures under management of Major Pond.

1887   Lecturing carries him to Oregon. *Washington and His Country.*

1888   *The Critical Period.*

1889   *Beginnings of New England. War of Independence.*

1890   Lectures at Lowell Institute. *Civil Government in the United States.*

1891   *The American Revolution.*

1892   May, orator at the centennial anniversary of the discovery and naming of the Columbia River. Vacations in Alaska. *The Discovery of America.*

Chronology

1894 Receives master's, bachelor of laws, and doctor of laws degrees from the University of Pennsylvania; doctor of letters degree from Harvard. *Life of Youmans. History of the United States for Schools. Presidents of the United States* (with Carl Schurz).

1897 *Old Virginia and Her Neighbors.*

1899 *A Century of Science. The Dutch and Quaker Colonies in America. Through Nature to God.*

1900 Invitation to take part in the King Alfred celebration in Winchester, England. *The Mississippi Valley in the Civil War.*

1901 July 4, dies at Gloucester, Massachusetts. July 7, buried in Petersham.

1902 Posthumous works published in 1902 and later, notably *New France and New England.*

CHAPTER *1*

As the Twig Is Bent

THE great theme of evolution which so thoroughly and strongly dominated the life and thinking of John Fiske has had its influence also on the modern student of Fiske; our twentieth-century thinking is almost automatically grounded not only in evolution but also in environmental psychology and ecology. As a result, there is a danger that we may tend to read too much into Fiske's background. Yet it does seem to be basically true that the portrait of the man clearly reflects the heredity and environment which shaped the boy. In a nation long cited as a "melting pot," we forget the homogeneity which existed in New England into the nineteenth century. At least in the northeast corner, the United States was heavily colonized by Englishmen; and John Fiske is a striking example of this fact. Descended in almost every branch from men and women who were not only English, but largely upper middle class, and Puritan from the days of the Reformation, he was born into a strongly unified atmosphere. It is true that his father's people were not New Englanders, but they, too, were English and of Quaker persuasion. His father's early death ended any direct influence that might have come from that quarter.

Although John Fiske clashed with orthodoxy while still a youth, his inborn need for religious belief was deep enough to lead eventually to his major difference from his philosophical master, Herbert Spencer: the inescapable urge to reconcile science and religion; somehow to make his scientific view of life conclude in an unshakable acceptance of God and His majestic plan. In this respect, Fiske reflected far more the American attitude of Ralph Waldo Emerson and Theodore Parker than the English view of Spencer. More than anything

13

else in Fiske's life, it was undoubtedly the quiet pressure of firm faith on the part of his grandmother and his mother that fixed in him such a solid emotional and spiritual need.

Middletown, Connecticut, in the middle years of the nineteenth century, was certainly a spot to reinforce the characteristics of the family influence. In fact, it would be difficult to determine for the Fisk family which was the chicken and which the egg: the Fisks and Middletown belonged together as completely as Sunday and sermons. And Middletown just before the Civil War is an excellent example of a unified background. The days of great shipping and some cosmopolitan flavor had passed; the new industrialism had not yet come. At the time of Fiske's birth, it was a town of some ten thousand people, many of whom were descendants of colonial merchants, shipowners, and traders. The memory, as well as some of the prosperity, lingered; but what John Fiske remembered many years later was the attempt to reclaim greatness through the railroad.

"Among the topics of discussion on which my youthful years were nourished, along with predestination and original sin and Webster's Seventh of March Speech, a certain preeminence was assumed by the Airline Railroad." Although he found this question more abstruse and perplexing than any of the others, he recalled that its advocates painted the future in rose color, while to its adversaries the gloom it foretold "would make the blackest midnight cheerful."[1] Indeed, the impression must have been great for, ever afterward, he was fascinated by the railroads and was vitally aware of the part they played in the material progress of the United States. When he was a boy, however, his concern was on a more homely level: he would return to school in Stamford, he told his mother, "on the cars; to go by boat costs just twice as much."[2] This observation was born far more of New England thrift than of adverse economic circumstances.

Despite the remaining cosmopolitan flavor and the differences of opinion about the Airline Railroad, there was a heavily unified political and religious outlook revealing the basic homogeneity of the town, perhaps of even the entire state of Connecticut. Writing from Stamford, John sent a message to his step-grandfather in 1856: "Tell Mr. Lewis that the general opinion here is, that if Fillmore or Buchanan should be elected instead of Frémont, we shall be ruled by Paddies and Dutchmen for the next four years."[3] Such an attitude is an outgrowth of the views of an earlier generation cited in Fiske's essay on Jefferson: "I have heard my grandmother tell how old ladies in Connecticut, at the news of his election, hid their family Bibles. . . ."[4]

Such memories were reason enough for Fiske in adult years to inveigh strongly against provincialism and its narrowing influences. But what was to count more directly as the cause of his open rebellion was the religious picture of his youth, for the political seems to have slipped beneath the surface and affected him more fully than he consciously realized. The Sabbath was duly respected, and social recognition depended upon church membership. All of the town's six churches were not only Protestant and evangelical, but conservative as well. Wesleyan University added much to the cultural life of the town; but, like most American institutions of higher learning of the era, it was church dominated and so not likely to furnish much contrast or conflict. And the position of the Fisks in the town tended to strengthen not only the religious but the social and economic upper middle classness; his grandfathers had been town clerks for generations.

An insistence on environment can, of course, be carried too far; Fiske himself would have placed the weight on heredity. Obviously, John Fiske was not the only boy growing up in Middletown during these years, and all of his compatriots surely did not grow into men who had been poured from a mold. And we are instantly reminded of Tom Sawyer, whose response to a comparable background (a predominantly female and orthodox household in a quiet, small town) was one of good-natured revolt. There is, indeed, much of Tom Sawyer in John Fiske. Without question, different personalities respond in their own way to the same or similar environments. Nevertheless, an initial emphasis on background goes a long way toward providing an insight into Fiske both as a man and as a writer. By temperament he was a person particularly responsive to the world around him—we would not want to say either in a chameleonlike or weak-willed fashion—but he was certainly sensitive to outward conditions, both physical and intellectual. Nor is the allusion to Mark Twain without reason. Roughly of the same generation, both of these men faced the challenge and the problems of Victorian America; each in his way became a spokesman and interpreter of that age; and the eventually diverging responses of each to the Victorian dilemma reveal much about each as an individual.

I *Family*

On March 30, 1842, a son was born to Mary (Fisk Bound) and Edmund Brewster Green, in Middletown, Connecticut. The boy was christened Edmund Fisk Green. His mother, as has already been indicated, was from a long-established Middletown family. His father had been a student at Wesleyan University but had left in his senior year to spend two years reading law with Judge Storrs. In 1840, the father became editor of the *New England Review,* a weekly Whig journal published in Hartford; and he soon married his college sweetheart. Three years later, seeking better opportunities in journalism and Whig politics, Green moved to New York City. In 1849, with the inauguration of Zachary Taylor, he moved on to Washington.

If the opinions of the family and the Connecticut party leaders are to be accepted, Edmund Green deserved political preferment. But the realities and conflicts of the "spoils system" denied him recognition of any sort greater than service as private secretary to Senator Henry Clay. Whether this experience played a part in his son's later disapproval of "civil service" we can only guess, but more immediately Green's political future, plus the developments related to the California gold rush, led him at the end of 1850 to Panama. Apparently, Edmund Green had something of the practical man as well as the adventurer in his nature, for he remained in Panama and established a weekly newspaper—a more sensible plan than trying his luck in the goldfields. That this plan was predetermined rather than a mere seizing of opportunity is indicated by a letter from young Edmund to his grandmother Green in May, 1850, in which he says that he hopes to visit his father's family "before we go to South America."[5] What vast difference might have been made in the life of the son can be only conjecture since Edmund Green the elder contracted cholera and died in Panama in July, 1852.

Mary Green, who had followed her husband to New York, had remained there during all of these attempts by her husband to establish the fortunes of the young family. The boy, however, except for short visits with his parents, had remained with his grandmother in Middletown. With his mother's second marriage to Edwin Wallace Stoughton in 1855, young Edmund elected to remain with his grandmother in Middletown and soon, at her request, changed his name legally to John Fisk.[6]

When John was three, his grandmother remarried, so that the household in which he grew up consisted of his grandparents, Mr. and Mrs. Elias Lewis, and Mr. Lewis' daughter by a previous marriage, Sallie. It was a quiet, adult household in which a good deal more attention was paid to the youngster's learning than to any boisterousness typical of boyhood. Perhaps, too, John had a bit more attention focused on him than was entirely good for him. That most of this attention came from the feminine side of the family may be inferred from the positive actions of his mother, grandmother, and Sallie, as well as from the negative fact that he never referred to his steprelatives by any name other than Mr. Stoughton and Mr. Lewis.

Still, the portrait of the precocious and bookish boy who shunned the rough and tumble of other boys has been too sharply etched already in black and white. And Fiske himself contributed no little to this portrait, especially in the long autobiographical letter written in 1862 to the girl he was courting. But here he was, legitimately enough, romanticizing. A careful reading of the letters written during his boyhood shows that this portrait is essentially accurate but does need some modification, some coloring. On the one hand, there are reports to his mother of normal boyish activities. He belonged to a club and was elected its president. He went skating, rowing, wading, and nutting in the proper seasons. One report of such activity shows clearly both the boy and the young scholar: "we got our pockets full of walnuts and sat down under the pines to eat them. And we amused ourselves wading about in the Sebethe River, half-way out to Meridan Mountain" and he promptly adds the characteristic note, "the river at this point is 40 feet wide and 4 feet deep in the middle."[7] John also had a carpentry shop of his own where he built a model frigate which won a prize. Later, while at Harvard, he clearly became involved in student affairs, despite his reputation as "a grind." And, in his later life, John Fiske was a gregarious, outgoing man, one much in need of friends and a social life—even if we must note that there is a kind of unconscious class distinction, more intellectual than social, in his choice of friendships.

On the other hand, we do have to admit an early tendency in Fiske to be concerned with books and ideas more than with play. He set his heart on a Greek-English dictionary which his grandmother felt to be somewhat expensive; and, to buy it, John began to earn the money himself by selling old bones to an Irishman named Hennessy at thirty-seven cents a barrel. He had built up the sum of $3.40 when Mrs. Lewis capitulated and made up the difference. While Fiske cannot be said to rival John Stuart Mill in brilliance, there is little doubt that he early proved himself to be an advanced if not a precocious student. But even here his tendency was to follow paths which intrigued him—a larger interest, almost of a romantic kind—in knowledge itself rather than in the formalities of education through the schools. Whatever the area might be, from the simple fact of helping the local seamstress in making him a vest to the study of the cosmos itself, John was at his best in following the typical Yankee pattern of trying to discover how things worked. In his writing this same quality appears in the more formal guise of seeking out patterns of cause and effect. In later years Fiske always seemed a bit sensitive about his academic standing and his scholarly reputation, perhaps subconsciously acknowledging a temperament which more often followed its desires than its academic duty. For I do not think it unjust, despite his contemporary reputation, to assert that, in the final analysis, John Fiske's scholarship proved to be amazingly wider and more dramatic than it was deep.

II *The Young Scholar*

However we may alter the description overdrawn in the eulogies closely following Fiske's death, there can be no doubt that the young scholar was more than adequately prepared when he entered Betts Academy in Stamford in the spring of 1855. By tutoring at home, reading on his own, and study with a Mr. Brewer, John had grounded himself well in arithmetic, Latin, Greek, logic, composition, and declaration. His grades with Brewer are an indication of a student who demonstrated above-average ability. Yet it must be kept in mind that this list closely follows the curriculum of the day; and a true evaluation of his youthful intellectual prowess must, therefore, be measured in terms of class standing, not by the subject matter which looks so weighty to moderns. Without denigrating the true value of his scholarship, it is still necessary to remember that proficiency in these subjects was not unusual at the time and that the method of teaching them measured largely the student's capacity for memorizing and reciting.

For instance, John's letters very early are filled with a kind of irrelevant factual matter often used today as newspaper filler. One letter to his mother begins: "By my geography of 1850, London is 2,520,000 inhabitants,"[8] and a little later he includes an encyclopedic biography of Gottfried von Leibnitz which looks like a classroom exercise in composition. This material suggests that what can be truly regarded as a most competent, even outstanding, school record should not be expanded into a stupendous intellectual performance through a failure to realize that educational patterns and methods have changed since John Fiske's school days. Using the same standards of measurement, one finds his achievements at Betts following a consistent pattern: he was valedictorian of his class and won first prize in the graduation-day oratorical exercise for an address, "Silent Influence," but there is no indication from him or from Mr. Betts that here stood a child prodigy. This kind of claim is as unfair a judgment as the reverse would be; it demands too much of the rest of his performance in life.

III *Religious and Scientific Thought*

Nor, to anyone who has taught boys and young men, does there seem to be any need for elaborate explanation of his religious development. As J. S. Clark says, "religion came as wholly in the natural order of things."[9] Under the influence of home and school, John joined the orthodox North Congregational Church in his home town. And as horizons grew, bringing him into contact with the scientific thought of the day, he found less and less satisfaction in that church. Like so many earnest young men, he sought for answers which religion simply cannot give and was disappointed when the reality failed to measure up to the ideal in religious education. Like so many young men from small towns, he found the narrow, old-fashioned view of aging ministers an irritation which accentuated the failure of religion. It is a situation through which young people usually pass, and yet we must note that the crisis was particularly acute for an age on the verge of Darwin's theories of evolution. Many young men were savoring the doubts raised by the new science: Huxley, Alfred Wallace, William James, Henry and Brooks Adams, and later Jack London, Theodore Dreiser, and others in their turn.

Perhaps the feature which gives individuality to young John's religious crisis is his own temperament. He was neither one to remain silent nor to be dishonest with himself or others, and he therefore spoke out loudly and clearly when he found himself moving away from the beliefs of his family and his town. The terms of his admission are a little amusing though this makes the situation no less painful: "In her sore perplexity grandma asked me whether I believed in the Bible, meaning whether I believed everything in it; of course I said no. I couldn't lie even to save her feelings. She felt rather bad about it. She asked me if I didn't believe Christ was God, and of course, again I had to say no. How can a man have two natures without having two medulla oblongatas? A double ego, a double centre of innervation is something to which I cannot yet subscribe."[10]

In fact, when this confession was finally made, it brought not only a great relief to him but an attempt to convert his mother to his new way of thinking. No wonder the family was upset and the clergyman impatient; this view was not easy to accept from a lad of eighteen. Yet always he was sincerely torn between the pain of acting a lie and that of hurting his grandmother. It is this polite but firm refusal to compromise which gave him the reputation of "village infidel." A deeper understanding of youth or of the changes taking place in thought, on the part of the church, might have helped; but it was the day when young people were seen and not heard rather than the day of young people's groups. And for that matter, theology had its back to the wall—or thought it did. The Reverend Mr. Taylor and his colleagues knew only too well that there were changes in thought: Satan was abroad again in the land as he had been in the days of Salem witch-craft. A less painful but less honest willingness to give lip-service would have made for less drama, but Fiske was feeling his oats. By the time of his rejection of the church, he had his sights on college and was already deep in that other phase of young manhood—the awareness of how little his elders knew.

Meanwhile, the schooling at Betts Academy was aimed directly, as far as John Fiske was concerned, at gaining entrance to Yale University. For various reasons, including the strain on his health that might result from too intensive study, it was decided that further preparation would be of value before he took the college entrance examinations. For this purpose, his family chose the newly opened school of the Reverend Henry Colton in Middletown. John's first reaction to Colton and to his school was one of intense dislike and scorn; he shrewdly fell back on the argument of expense to dissuade his family: "His price is stupendous—perfectly alarming: $40. for three months schooling! Mr. Chase would be only $8. That was his price when I used to go to him; it can't be much more now."[11] But the family was assured that Colton had more influence at Yale than even good entrance-examination scoring, so his grandmother was, for once, adamant.

Within three days, John discovered that Mr. Colton was no fool. In fact, it would not be exaggerating to say that Colton's method was responsible for the first awakening of Fiske's real talents. Mr. Colton insisted on smooth flowing translations of Greek, the only way which can lead to a true appreciation of the beauty of literature; and, whatever may have been Fiske's judgments later, it is true that an esthetic response to literature was his notable characteristic. Colton did him a great service in opening this approach. Later, it may be difficult for the student of Fiske to distinguish among esthetic, emotional, and even sentimental qualities in his work; however, we shall see that Fiske's thought and living are strongly colored, perhaps dominated, by those aspects of personality which may generally be classified as feelings.

Mr. Colton also insisted on what was called "theming"—the tracing of words in a Greek passage so as to find and give the corresponding word in Latin, Hebrew, Sanskrit, German, and sometimes French. Again, the method could not have been better had it been tailored for John Fiske personally; for we find in it the foundation for his exploration of philology; and comparative philology was the opening wedge into the exploration of evolutionary theory, philosophy, and history. The proposed few weeks with Colton lengthened into two years. Fiske continued to dislike his mentor personally, but he willingly admitted that he had learned much; and, with characteristic optimism, he shifted his goal from that of being one of Yale's youngest freshmen to that of being so well prepared that he would be valedictorian of his class. "For a Yale valedictorian is immortalized!"[12]

During these years of growing pains and growing pleasures there was a good deal of wide and sound reading—Milton, Shakespeare, Emerson, Theodore Parker. Outstanding was Alexander von Humboldt's *The Cosmos* (1845-62) in its encouragement to widen the horizons to take in nothing less than all cosmic phenomena. "Do you not consider Humboldt the greatest man of the nineteenth century, and the most erudite that ever lived? Does not the 'Cosmos' exhibit more vast learning than any other uninspired book?"[13] John Fiske dealt in superlatives, and a little later the accolade passed to Spencer. Much of his lighter reading at this time was the fiction of Charles Dickens; indeed, the Dickens world became as real to Fiske as the actual world.

During these years also began the development of another outlet of expression. His grandmother acquired a piano; and, with his Yankee curiosity to know how things worked, John taught himself to play. He knew how to read and write music and became sufficiently proficient on the piano to play such works as Mozart's Twelfth Mass. This ability, plus his training in the church choir, led eventually to musical compositions of his own which, at least in the judgment of John Knowles Paine, had some merit. Fiske's own musical favorites were German *lieder*, which provided not only a means of recreation but added to his attractiveness as a lecturer. Somewhat as Dickens found not only a personal outlet but a wider audience appeal for his books in his dramatic readings, so Fiske later combined informal vocal and piano recitals with his lecturing. Young ladies who had not quite grasped the import of the lecture could be deeply affected by the romance or sentiment of his music.

In July, 1859, the preparation for Yale was at an end, and

John passed his examinations to enter as a freshman. Possibly he wore his learning a trifle self-consciously: "I missed only one question and that was in arithmetic. A tutor asked me to find the present worth of a sum of money. I told him I was not prepared on mercantile problems. He smiled and gave me a sum in the square root of decimals which I did."[14] About two weeks later he wrote to his mother setting forth the greater advantages of Harvard; the letter continues an argument which obviously had been opened at an earlier date about postponing entrance still another year and attending Harvard instead of Yale. It seems fairly safe to say that this switch was not so rapid as it might at first appear. We suspect that he felt it a duty to his conscience and to his family to complete the application for Yale—to prove that he was indeed ready for college. Possibly Fiske was already experiencing a feeling which echoes through later letters—a need to prove to his stepfather that he was a capable and dependable person. Whether Mr. Stoughton ever directly expressed a doubt that John might prove something of a drifter or a dilettante has not been recorded.

Whatever may have been the facts of family relationships, it is also evident that the desire to change colleges was largely governed by the break with religion. John felt a need to get out into the world, and Yale was not only a citadel of orthodoxy but too close to home. This recognition is reflected in the argument Fiske gives his mother for the new plan: "The course at Harvard is very different and much harder. . . . It is true that the instruction at Harvard is conducted with less strictness than at Yale. It is a bad place for a careless scholar, but unequalled in facilities for an ambitious one."[15] These are the good reasons, but underlying are the real reasons: Harvard offered more work in languages and science, gave more latitude in choosing electives, and was apparently freer thinking theologically.

And deeper than all of these reasons lay a sense of non-compatibility. Reviewing the history of the Great Awakening in *New France and New England,* Fiske made statements which can legitimately be read as interpretations arising from personal experience. That he is making use of such a method is suggested by his own comment: "But if we come forward into the nineteenth century, it can hardly be denied that while both states have maintained a high intellectual level, Massachusetts has been the more liberal-minded community."[16] Thus, through the history of religion in Connecticut and his observations on the founding of Yale, Fiske revealed something of what lay beyond his decision to switch—not that he was consciously aware of this reason as a boy about to enter college. Still, he must have sensed then what he described later: "Now this founding of Yale College exerted a conservative effect on the mind of Connecticut. While on the one hand it brought a classical education within the reach of many persons who would not have gone to Cambridge to get it, on the other hand it tended to cut off the clergy of Connecticut from the liberalizing forces which were so plainly beginning to be powerful at Harvard. From the outset something like a segregation began...."[17] The more immediate reasons for going to Harvard are transmuted to a different level.

After Mr. and Mrs. Stoughton gave their consent to the change, John settled down to long months of intensive study designed to prepare him for taking examinations and entering Harvard with advanced standing; he was aiming for the sophomore or junior level. This time he planned and executed his program of study by himself, with some aid from a tutor in geometry. Four times a week he recited to Joseph Ellis in this subject. In addition to the formal study program he laid out a double-barreled reading program, half of which was review for college subjects and the other half in all the scientific works he could lay his hands on. His letters are so full of this reading that there could scarcely be time for anything else—except the walk he took each evening with his friend George Roberts (and even that was to compare notes on reading as much as for bodily exercise). Whenever Fiske became involved in a project, he was capable of hurling himself into a prodigious amount of work; it is no wonder that his teachers had warned him about endangering his health with too close application to his books.

In May, 1860, Fiske left Middletown for Cambridge. What a shaking of heads there must have been, especially vigorous on the part of Dr. Taylor, the family clergyman, who had seen the last of the Fiskes turned infidel. Above all other causes, Rev. Taylor held responsible the wicked books John had been permitted to read. Poor Grandmother Lewis had proudly displayed them as evidence that John was a good and faithful student. On the northward journey John may have felt an exhilaration at being on his own, the determination to prove to his mother and grandmother that he was worthy of the love and devotion they had given, and the sense of escape from the home town. But like most boys who go away to school, he soon discovered how much home had meant. And he had not escaped to religious freedom; Harvard may have been more liberal than Yale, but it was no more prepared to relax requirements for attendance at chapel nor to accept the recently published ideas of Charles Darwin without a struggle. Even alumnus Ralph Waldo Emerson was officially persona non grata in the halls of Cambridge because of his religious notions.

CHAPTER 2

Harvard, Fair Harvard

I *The Student Years*

TWO factors played a large part in determining the pattern of Fiske's career at Harvard. First, he started off on the right foot socially. An initial confusion when he discovered that the tutor he had engaged was not prepared to help him work toward advanced standing led Fiske to apply to an old friend of Mr. Stoughton, Judge Benjamin R. Curtis, who helped John locate the proper tutor, made him welcome to his family circle, introduced him to Harvard's President Felton; and, most important, also introduced him to his partner, George Ticknor. This was, indeed, starting at the top both socially and academically, for Ticknor graciously placed his library at the young man's disposal.

The second factor was the rapidly developing scientific bent of Fiske's mind accompanied by the rejection of formal and orthodox religion. To see the extent to which his thinking had gone, it is worthwhile to turn back and review briefly those last few months in Middletown. Fiske's reading, ostensibly designed for taking entrance examinations had, as usual, proceeded along diverse lines. A number of historical and scientific works, including Humboldt, George Grote, Edward Gibbon, Darwin, Louis Agassiz, Asa Gray, and most importantly Buckle's *History of Civilization in England,* raised a great many questions for which, for John Fiske at least, a battery of standard theological works provided no answers.

The contrast between Buckle and the Reverend Taylor was too much, for Buckle "led him to focus his thought upon the important part played by nature in the development of civilized man, and upon the need of a philosophy which should present the objective world of phenomena as revealed by science and

26

the subjective world of human consciousness as revealed by civilization in harmony with some universal principle which could absorb both in unity or purpose."[1] But the Reverend Taylor shudderingly ignored science and sermonized upon a vision from eternity: "A multitude of angels enter singing 'Holy, Holy, Lord God Almighty'—but the scene changes. Envy enters into the breast of the mightiest of that angel host. He asserts his dominion against the Father. Consternation reigns in Heaven; but Christ sent by Jehovah hurls in holy wrath and God-like vengeance that rebel host to Hell."[2] Jonathan Edwards had preached this sort of thing more powerfully, and it had made beautiful poetry from the pen of John Milton; but it was of no comfort to a young man swept away on visions of the new science.

In Middletown, the Reverend Taylor had conscientiously tried to reconvert John Fiske. The latter had asked for excommunication: "You see where I stand: why not expell me from the church?" But the minister replied: "That we cannot do unless you commit some gross act of immorality." "That," said John, "I pray God I may never do."[3] Even at his most skeptical, Fiske never saw the universe as either immoral or amoral—he never doubted a basic morality. He appealed to his mother to try to see his reasoning: "I can appreciate why Grandma Lewis might find it impossible to grasp my ideas—but you are younger than she, and consequently know more, for a person brought up between 1820 and 1840 will know more than one brought up between 1795 and 1815, unless the latter is extraordinary."[4] A curious argument, it is one Fiske retained throughout his life; this early he is already making the assumption that civilization moves in a straight line, from generation to generation, slowly amassing knowledge from the universe. He concludes with an appeal to emotion: "Besides if Christian doctrine is true, what becomes of your son and both your husbands?"[5] Clearly, all three were "sinners in the hands of an angry God." At least, for the youngest of them, Taylor thought so; for, by revealing Fiske's position to members of the congregation, he tried to bring community pressure to bear to rescue the young infidel.

This attempt led only to social disapproval, but at least two friends had understood. One, the Reverend John L. Dudley, was a Congregationalist minister of liberal views. The other friend, George Litch Roberts, a Wesleyan student, became John's lifelong friend. Roberts was also regarded as an infidel, and it was he who brought Buckle's *History* for John to read. It may well have been Roberts' decision to move on to Harvard for postgraduate professional studies that focused Fiske's attention on Cambridge.

The atmosphere of Harvard and Cambridge in 1860 was designed to increase challenge rather than to settle doubts. Fiske's first encounter with religion was innocuous enough—a visit to Boston's King's Chapel with the Curtis family where John mistook a Unitarian sermon for an Episcopalian one and was less impressed by the service than by the music, "consisting mostly of old anthems of Crotch, Purcell, and others, composed before Handel had founded the modern school."[6] At the college, the forces of religion were still officially dominant; but the lines of battle were beginning to form. President Felton was a thoroughgoing Classicist and a conservative. Professor Bowen, of philosophy, had been among the leaders of the Unitarian forces when the earlier split had come with the Transcendentalists, and he was no more willing to give ground to science. Asa Gray, professor of botany, taking the position that Fiske was to argue so thoroughly, had already given the opinion that Darwin's hypothesis merely attributed a different mode and time to divine agency. His colleague, Louis Agassiz, on the other hand, continued to reject Darwin on scientific grounds; and, for the moment, his view held with most theologians and many scientists. Because their courses were advanced and elective for the most part, Gray and Agassiz were not in direct contact with younger students. Such a combination, which cost John Fiske a good deal in later years, stirred the minds of thinking students, but did not permit freedom of discussion.

An incident which can be read as a clue to the future came even before he had taken his entrance examinations. Poking about the Old Corner Bookshop about a month after his arrival in Cambridge, Fiske came upon a notice of a proposed publication of Spencer's system of philosophy to be sold by subscription. To Roberts, he wrote at once: "Oh George, my soul is on fire! (to use a favorite expression of Horace) ... My name goes down tomorrow—subscription only $2.50 a year." And to his mother, "I hope Mr. Stoughton will subscribe. I consider it my duty to mankind as a Positivist to subscribe; and if I had $2,000,000 I would lay $1,000,000 at Mr. Spencer's feet to help him execute his great work."[7] From the phrasing, it is evident that Fiske had read something of Spencer already; but here was to be the most exciting venture of his life—and the foundation for his later wonderful association with Spencer himself.

At the end of August, there were three days of written and oral examinations which Fiske passed most respectably; he was admitted as a sophomore without conditions. During the next four years, there is in his letters some complaint about the narrow formality of the curriculum and, to a large extent, this criticism was justified. The basic departments were still the age-old classics—mathematics, history, and rhetoric and oratory; electives were available but on a carefully limited basis. On the other hand, college students in all generations are notoriously anxious to deal with contemporary thought and are constantly asking for "off-beat" curricula. And Harvard was noted for a comparatively liberal curriculum which included departments of modern languages, physics, chemistry and mineralogy, natural history, and anatomy and physiology, as well as philosophy.

Among the noted scholars on the faculty were James Russell Lowell, Francis Bowen, Asa Gray, Louis Agassiz, and Francis Child. If Fiske could later write, "I am clear that I owe absolutely nothing to Harvard except the friendships formed while there,"[8] the failure lay more in the educational method than in either faculty or curriculum. This method, which Harvard shared with her sister institutions, was described rather accurately by the Reverend Frederic Hedge: "The college proper is simply a more advanced school for boys, not differing essentially in principle and theory from the public schools in all our towns. In this, as in those, the principle is coercion. Hold your subject fast in one hand and pour knowledge into him with the other. The Professors are task-masters and police-officers—the President the chief of college police."[9] The reference to police officers alluded more to religious rules than to academics; there was, of course, a strong emphasis on at least formal recognition of religion with required chapel and church attendance. But there was also a conscious awareness of the new ideas, especially the battle over Darwinism in which Gray and Agassiz had publicly lined up on opposite sides.

As a matter of fact, this battle between science and religion occupied a good deal more of the attention of the college—or at least of student John Fiske—than the more immediate problems of the Civil War. In 1861, he defended his indifference to Roberts: "What fools people make of themselves about this confounded war! Why I forget there is a war half the time. What's war when a fellow has 'Kosmos' on his shelf and 'Faust' on his table?"[10] There is a good deal more than petulance in the outburst: not only did Fiske see a possible disruption of the peaceful pursuit of his studies, but he knew with reasonable surety that his eyesight was sufficiently bad to keep him from serving had he been impelled in that direction. However, in 1862, with Lincoln's Emancipation Proclamation and the challenge to the president's war powers, Fiske was thoroughly aroused. In September, he wrote to his fiancée: "I hope that the fiendish institution of slavery, which has hitherto made me ashamed of America, is at last to fall. I always was a red-hot anti-slavery man in principle, but never cared much for the success of a war that was to leave us on this question just where we were before." But, a month later, he asserted: "Of course I do not hold any opinions but such as are founded on purely scientific principles. I am not an abolitionist. . . . No one can start from 'Social Statics' and logically deduce conclusions which shall be other than unfavorable to the South at present."[11] However he may have stood on the issues involved, the military campaigns captured his imagination. Following the tides of battle in the New York *Daily Times*, he worked out each day's operations by attaching pins with colored heads to huge maps posted on his wall.

In retrospect, we are apt to remember our college lives as acted out against the background of great world events. At the time, however, each of us was more likely absorbed almost completely in the day-to-day student life. A portrait of John Fiske from this angle would show a somewhat thin young man rather generally known to his colleagues as a "squirt" or "bookworm." His stepfather would have had no trouble in recognizing the portrait since John's one great dissipation was books. While he rather self-righteously pointed out that he was in no way wild, that his only sensual indulgences were his pipe and his mug of beer, John innocently overspent his allowance filling his library with great bargains that would "last a lifetime." Having run up tremendous book bills, he would engage in elaborate small economies for compensation: "Bessie Curtis asked me to go to Swampscott again Sunday but it costs rather too much, can't go 90 cents even for one of those visits, could get one of Didot's modern classics for one dollar, you know."[12]

Although the books thus purchased were certainly solid works, nevertheless a sensual pleasure is involved, since Fiske invariably was beguiled by beautifully bound copies. For John Fiske, it was possible to judge a book by its cover. Sir Charles Lyell, "beautiful in one-half calf brown, Dunglison in *one-half calf black*, marbled sides purple," and "Kosmos too in one-half green turkey, gold—O Lord, if you could see it! Michelet in one-half green calf, gilt tremendously, the richest of the lot!"[13] So he described his library to George Roberts that very first June in Cambridge.

To Roberts, Fiske also wrote of the furnishings of his room and his delight in them. These, too, indicate a richness of taste: "drapery curtains of brocatelle, red and gold with heavy tassels to loop up the sides onto gilt bunches of grapes which hold them back."[14] The draperies, of course, had been sent by his mother from the Stoughton's Fifth Avenue house, along with busts of Luther and Melanchthon (John would have "preferred Descartes and Liebnitz"), oil paintings and engravings, and elegant bibelots for his desk. While a boy cannot be held responsible for the way his parents choose to furnish his room away from home, the pleasure with which John lingers over the descriptions does indicate that he was generally pleased with his mother's selection; nor was such interior decoration standard operating procedure. By way of contrast, Oliver Wendell Holmes, Jr., whose father was then a professor in the medical school, also had lodgings away from home: "His room, bleak and uncarpeted, was nearly filled with a large featherbed, and warmed only by the open fire"[15]; and Holmes was of the same college generation as Fiske.

Without a doubt Fiske spent long hours in his comfortable room poring over the elegant volumes in his library; reading was his greatest joy. Nor is there any doubt from incidents he recounts in his letters that his classmates looked upon him as a scholar and a "grind." But the extent to which he cultivated and rather naïvely built up this reputation is not so easily determined. To see into the complexity of his motivations at this distance is impossible, but at least a part of John Fiske's nature demanded recognition from outside; for without an audience, he could not play his role. The letters are studded with alternating scornful remarks about the limitations of some of his classmates intellectually and with reports of "what splendid fellows" some of them are. "My room will not seem *quite* like home until I have seen some of my friends in it," he observes in his first report from Cambridge; and he balances the comment with "As he knows nothing about science he can never become very intimate with me, though I should say he was, on the whole, a noble fellow."[16] Fiske's need included not only a small circle of individual friends but at least a small share in the organization known as the college class. He bought a class cap when the individualists were making a point of not buying them. When his class engaged in a mock funeral bewailing the death of football—forbidden by the faculty—John was present. It was great fun and very elaborately conducted, but it certainly is not to be interpreted as any great, modern interest in athletics.

In Fiske's senior year he was elected an associate editor of the *Harvard Magazine*; and, in the end, as class poet, he produced the class ode. Like most class poets, he played this last role with a touch of wry humor: "I think the Ode is perfectly diabolical, but as a first—and I hope a *last*—attempt, perhaps it is no worse than college songs usually are, that is my sole consolation. It took me exactly one hour to write it, which is at the rate of 3 minutes a line, that would be rather slow for writing prose. I could never write an essay at that rate."[17] In short, John Fiske took sufficient part in student activities for his role to serve as a foundation for a fond alumnal attachment to his "class," especially when some of its members came forward with hearty support of his lecture programs some twenty years after graduation.

Above all, he was a young man romantically and unconsciously playing a role: he was the young rebel, the prophet; he would not lead but would point the way quietly and through reason. It is not foreshadowing too much or taking advantage of hindsight to see him as already dreaming of himself as the living example of the right path—as destined to be a memorable figure in showing mankind the way to progress. And, in all humility, for there is no personal credit in such fame, he had only to follow the clarity of reason. When other men had been shown the truth, they would inevitably follow. When somewhat older and somewhat wiser, he would wistfully realize how difficult a task this leadership was; in his admiration for Alexander Hamilton, he noted: "Hamilton's style was a direct appeal to man's reason; and the wonder of it was that he could accomplish by such a direct appeal what most men cannot accomplish without calling into play the various arts of the rhetorician."[18] Basically, Fiske could now, as later, have borrowed a phrase from Henry Adams in that his education also was from the eighteenth-century Enlightenment—though Fiske was far more of a romantic moralist.

The portrait is not complete without at least sketching in several major events in some detail: John's visit to Ralph Waldo Emerson, his public admonition and near expulsion from college, and his one and only love affair. The visit to Emerson seems to have come about more or less by accident. Fiske was asked to accompany his friend Edward McCarthy to Lexington to see about a teaching job. Nothing being available there, they were advised to go on to Concord and consult with Mr. Emerson. At first, Fiske was a trifle awed, but Emerson welcomed the young men warmly and invited them to tea. They were quickly enchanted and overwhelmed: "I did not expect to find him so booked on science but I find him tremendously so. I was astonished not only at his learning but also at the wisdom which lurked in everything he said, and at his goodness. I have never before seen a man whose works have made him immortal and I listened to him as to an oracle. I thought him the greatest man I ever saw." Emerson entertained his visitors with stories about Carlyle and Theodore Parker; impressed them with the great man's knowledge of Buckle, Marie Bichat, and Voltaire; and charmed them by his rich bass voice: "I felt as much at home with him as I would with an old acquaintance; there was something so charming, so simple and unaffected and exquisitely-bred about him. . . . Of all the men I ever saw, none can be compared with him for depth, for scholarship, and for attractiveness —at least so I think."[19] Although Fiske was given to superlatives, the visit must have made a deep impression; there is a good

deal more of Emersonian thinking in John Fiske than has been
generally recognized. It was, indeed, an experience for a college
sophomore, and well might he have begun his letter home,
"Yesterday was a day I shall never forget."

The threat to Fiske's college career came, as might be expected, from the forced lip-service to religion. For all of his
quietness, Fiske was not a man to keep his opinions to himself;
and he had the reputation of knowing his Darwin too well
and for holding the heretical views of Emerson and Theodore
Parker. As a result, the Parietal Committee of the faculty had
an eye on him and in October of his junior year caught him
reading a volume of Auguste Comte in church. When questioned
by President Felton, John was not averse to attempting to
instruct even him in the modern way of thinking. He could
not resist the opportunity to set forth his ideas even if his
academic career would be endangered. John was polite enough:
he frankly admitted that he could see the insult, not intended
but still present, in reading during service. For that, he freely
apologized and promised that it would not happen again. But on
his real error, the holding of unorthodox views, he gave no
ground whatever. In all sweet reason he could not—and he
narrowly escaped suspension. Technically, the president's
grounds for objection were not so much the beliefs themselves
as John's willingness to try to convert his colleagues.

What Fiske did not know but what Felton and Bowen, if not
others on the faculty, had surely not forgotten was that Harvard
had had a similar experience in Emerson's time. The problem
in Fiske's undergraduate days was further accentuated by the
fact that Darwinism was not merely an academic question. Harvard was governed by the Massachusetts General Court, and in
the fall of 1860 Louis Agassiz had just succeeded in completing
a museum of comparative zoology. He had fought hard for
funds. "What," one of the members of the court demanded,
"has Agassiz with his pickled periwinkles and his polypuses
done that is really useful?" A liberal member answered bravely:
"The religious world owes the professor a debt of gratitude
for triumphantly combatting that new-fangled and monstrous
teaching that we are descended from monkeys." "I thank God,"
the first speaker roared, "that I have only to go to His word—
not to any French professor of atheism—for that!"[20] Innocents

rush in—and it's no wonder that President Felton was wary of precocious young men like John Fiske. If the ideas were reported to parents, there might indeed be repercussions in the legislature. No wonder either that Professor Bowen voted for suspension; he was experienced at attacking young atheists. Fiske's escape with a mere public admonition was a pure legality. The specifically stated grounds of offense had been only the question of reading in church, and Professor Peabody staunchly argued that it would be a disgrace to the college to suspend a good student only for that, especially since he had so handsomely apologized. A bare majority of the faculty concurred.

Of the views themselves, it would have done little good to deny his position; in the same month as his admonition, he had completed an article reviewing the second volume of Buckle's *History*. The article was accepted and published by the *National Quarterly* in the December issue. A second article, "The Evolution of Language," was published in the *North American Review* in the autumn following Fiske's graduation. Not to pass over the significance of his first published works, these articles were indeed remarkable performances for a college student. The first of these essays Fiske republished in *Darwinism and Other Essays* in 1885 with the observation that the reader must remember that it expressed youthful views that the years had somewhat modified. Nevertheless, he set down in it the evolutionary theme which in one phase or another was to be the cornerstone, the foundation, of his intellectual achievement.

The essay is neatly constructed more or less like an extended syllogism which examines and comments on Buckle's logical argument step by step. Mainly, Fiske refuses to allow the separation of "moral truths" from "intellectual truths": all truths are intellectual, and all are absolute. Change comes only as science broadens our awareness of understood truths, and with this awareness comes progress in both intellectual and moral areas. Just as the greyhound inherits swiftness, so man inherits virtue or vice. Thus, at this early stage, we have several of Fiske's basic premises: that science, by definition, is the means of revealing absolute truth; that progress, both physical and moral, is inevitable; and that the writer's task is to "instruct and entertain." In a modern sense, Buckle is scarcely entertaining; but

Fiske's criteria are derived from the eighteenth century, which placed a somewhat different construction on the word.

In Fiske's second and more ambitious undertaking, his task was to apply Spencer's evolutionary system to the study of linguistics. His approach became standard for him and left him open to the charge of being merely a synthesizer or popularizer of other men's ideas. One of the achievements of the new study of philology in the early nineteenth century had been the classification of world languages into great families. Taking his linguistics from August Schleicher and Friedrich Müller, Fiske wove in his doctrine from Spencer to demonstrate that Schleicher's classification was not merely descriptive but was a developmental progression, with Chinese as the most primitive type of language and Indo-European as the most advanced and most civilized. Fiske argued that all languages had passed through these stages or would do so if they progressed. He felt that he "had found the key to all orderly processes of development; therefore, he tried to show that the scientifically verifiable laws of linguistics fitted his overall generalization and thus confirmed its validity."[21]

Perhaps right here we have a clue to John Fiske's entire career: the figure of a key. Spencer's system was the key, and with it Fiske went from philosophy and linguistics to history, unlocking and flinging open the doors. The key was as a gospel, and it was his duty to show how it might be concretely applied. He was, in fact, a minister without portfolio. Concretely, these two essays were important in that they came to the attention of Professor E. L. Youmans in New York, who had dedicated his life to spreading the gospel; and it was he who did so much to encourage Fiske and who brought Fiske and Spencer together. Without this initial impetus, we wonder what direction Fiske's career might have taken; for in a sense, these two essays and Youmans' response became a link in a chain similar to that in the nursery rhyme where the stick had to beat the dog before the old lady could get home at night. Fiske himself would have consented to the cause-and-effect sequence in this image.

With a love story, the biographer who depends on letters from one of the principals treads on doubly dangerous ground. It is always a temptation to read between the lines of personal letters, and with those as intimate as love letters this urge can even more quickly lead to misinterpretation. Nevertheless, if we take John Fiske's letters (the only evidence we have) at face value, we can still say that his meeting with Abby Morgan Brooks was the most significant event in Fiske's life.

Apparently it was love at first sight—or nearly so. Following a brief meeting in June, 1861, John expressed the hope that they might meet again in the autumn. When, in September, he learned that she planned to visit a brother in Chicago rather than come to Boston, he promptly got a week's leave of absence from school "to look for a teaching position" and visited the Brooks home in Petersham, Massachusetts. Clearly, he was already in love with Abby; in walking through the glorious Berkshire autumn from Athol, he fell in love with Petersham; and both loves were to last a lifetime. The entire Brooks family guessed at his first love; for, as John later sketched in events for his mother, he confessed that they had seen through his scheme: "Amazing episode—alone with James Brooks [Abby's brother]—'What on earth induced you to come to *Petersham* for a school?' said the old fox with a knowing look, 'there isn't much to call a man to such an out-of-the-way place unless there is something in it of *especial interest* to him.' I had the consummate cheek to smile and say, 'Well, that is just my case!' James grinned."[22]

Of the first view of Petersham Fiske writes: "As I climbed the long rise of road from Athol to the high plateau of Petersham every step revealed new beauties until at the summit I found before me a most impressive scene, on either side valleys with their long ridges of hills thickly wooded, rolling miles away into the distance. As I got nearer I paused to drink in the peace and loveliness of it all; the town lying so quietly before me, its church spires shining in the setting sun, wondering what these surroundings might have in store for me."[23]

By March, 1862, the engagement of Abby Morgan Brooks to John Fiske was announced; and now he was impatient to be done with college so that life might begin. His own family insisted that the marriage wait until he had some visible means of support and the major question now became what career to choose. His own preference seems to have been teaching; his family and, at first, his fiancée leaned toward the law. Among his classmates, John appears not to have been unusual in his indecision about choosing a career. "Among the one hundred and five graduates of 1863, fifty-seven had decided on their careers; of these twenty-one planned to become lawyers, sixteen to enter business, and thirteen to train as doctors"; four more had elected to teach and three to join the ministry.[24]

Fiske did not record his private thoughts, but it does not take too great a jump to perceive that his true choice was a literary career, a writer with a focus on linguistics. The inner vision must surely have been of himself as a great scholar writing down his lofty thoughts for the good of the human race. But he was a man in love, anxious to be married; and such a career was impossible without a private fortune. Adjusting his sights to the markets, Fiske saw teaching as the most rapid but dignified means to the end. Almost certainly his eye was on an eventual university position, possibly at Harvard; perhaps a passing thought was aimed at his stepfather's money. In any event, he almost secured a teaching position in Charlestown, but at the last moment it went to a man with experience.

This rejection was in September after his graduation, so it must have been with a touch of desperation that he submitted to the dreams of the family and agreed to study law. This meant more student days and further postponement of marriage, but no other course seemed to be open. As an incentive, his parents consented to his being married immediately upon his having been admitted to the bar. With such a goal in mind, Fiske's characteristic optimism took over, and he literally hurled himself into law studies and found them utterly fascinating. "I am perfectly enraptured, carried away and *electrified* with Blackstone," he wrote, and later, about Sir Henry Maine's *Ancient Law*, "It is perfectly GLORIOUS! I am going to read it over and over again until I know it by heart."[25] Not only was he reading his way through law, but he was also registered at the Harvard Law School, though he did little about attending classes.

As we might suspect, the attraction of the law to Fiske lay rather heavily on the philosophical and theoretical aspects of the subject rather than in its practical application. Nevertheless, in July, 1864, he took and passed the bar examinations and was admitted to the Massachusetts bar. On September 6, attorney John Fiske and Miss Brooks were joined in holy matrimony.

John Fiske had accomplished the tremendous task of completing studies in less than a year that Judge Curtis had assured him could not be managed in less than two.

II   *Search for a Career*

Some time after returning from his wedding journey, Fiske located office space and hung out his shingle. Although practice was diverted his way by his ever patient stepfather, any one who knew Fiske could have predicted that he was not to be a lawyer. During the anxious period when he had been awaiting the decision about the teaching position, he had indulged in an orgy of reading Sir Walter Scott's novels. In the midst of his law studies, he had received a visit from E. L. Youmans, whose kind recognition had added fuel to the dream of a literary career. At the same time, Charles Eliot Norton had taken over the *North American Review* and had personally asked Fiske to supply him with critical notices; there had not been time to read law and prepare full-dress essays or Norton might have asked for these as well. The appeal had led to two reviews: one on Mill's *Political Economy*, which Norton had accepted at once, the other on Youmans' *Chemistry*, which had been rejected but was shortly thereafter placed with the *Atlantic Monthly*.

We picture Lawyer Fiske dutifully taking care of the work offered by Mr. Stoughton, waiting for clients, and continuing to read widely in fiction, science, and history. His letters, while containing next to nothing about his law practice, were filled with comments on literary matters. He preferred John Lothrop Motley to William Prescott; Hawthorne's *Marble Faun* "is trash: *Scarlet Letter* is bearable." *Bleak House* is the greatest of Dickens' novels, though he adds solemnly that "The only blemish in the work is the death of old Krook in such an improbable way."[26] Thus it goes for several months with only one comment about his actual business in dozens of letters: "I have got a big case on hand now, my first case, one which will last a long time, if the old fools don't settle up, which I am afraid they will do, before I have made enough out of them."[27] This report, incidentally, appears in a letter written almost exactly one year after his admission to the bar. Add to all of this activity a pleasant correspondence with Herbert Spencer, one or two more book reviews accepted, and even Mr. Stoughton is going to be forced to admit that the law is not the answer.

It is difficult to come to a balanced judgment at this point. On the one hand, there is the fact that nothing can be more painful than a young man bound to one career while he longs for another. And there weighs on this side the great success that Fiske finally achieved. On the other hand, Fiske did not devote himself to making his law practice successful; the New England conscience apparently did not press him to prove himself before abandoning the field. Whichever way the scales tip, it is evident that one quality lacking in John Fiske's makeup was the sound business ability to manage his own financial affairs like a good Connecticut Yankee. What might have happened had he been forced from the beginning to pay his own way we cannot even surmise. Instead, by a curious kind of irony, there seems always to have been a sort of half-conscious fairy godmother just around the corner. Time and again throughout Fiske's life, usually at almost the last minute, a gift, an amazing deal with a publisher, a position with a salary but no heavy demands on his time would fall to Fiske's lot. Often it was all but too little and often almost too late, but always it kept alive his faith in the possibility of a literary career, and always it teased him to take the next step.

In the spring of 1866 the support must have come once again from his stepfather; for it was agreed that John was to withdraw from the law and see whether he could build on the reviews and his vast reading. Mr. and Mrs. Fiske and their little daughter Maud (born July, 1865) moved from Cambridge to grandmother's house in Middletown. Fiske's mood must have been indeed one of quiet desperation or of unbounded confidence to let him consent to such a move: he loved Cambridge dearly and, except for the family household, did not find the Middletown atmosphere congenial. In a sense, this period was one of exile.

Something of this feeling is caught in a letter, dated in September, to his brother-in-law, James Brooks: "Mr. Stoughton was a good deal stunned by my success in England. He has an idea that John Bull knows what's what, and won't lend countenance to poor writers. He is beginning to acquire a dim idea that my scientific labors mean something and to think that I may succed, after all, in my 'literary career' and that perhaps it will be well to get some of the credit of helping me along to distinction."[28]

It is highly probable that Fiske knew himself to be, as he then was, in the vanguard of a new movement. A staunch believer in the truth of the doctrine of evolution, he was not even gambling; he was sure that people would slowly be enlightened and that somehow his role was to be that of one of the leaders into the light. It was more in this mood that he had explained the move to Spencer earlier in June: "I have made the discovery that I am, as regards my constitutional relations to my environment, an idealist and not a realist; and that in order to accomplish anything *worthy* I must not seek to quit my ideal world. I have therefore come to a quiet country town where I expect to stay (alone with my books and my family) until some philological professorship or other place, which 'practical' men cannot fill shall take me away. I shall devote much time to acquiring a thorough knowledge of Sanskrit and Greek as the basis for future labors; and hope from time to time to write articles, as a means both of mental training and material support."[29]

However unpleasant in little details a retreat to Middletown might be, he retired there to marshal his forces, perhaps to survey the ground and map out his campaign as he had mapped the Civil War campaigns in his college room. That the new movement would sweep past him and leave him, paradoxically, to be recorded as fighting a rearguard action of the old guard, he could hardly have been expected to predict.

We are accustomed to think of a literary career in terms of what has come to be called "creative literature"—poetry, fiction, drama. Although John Fiske recorded no specific esthetic by which he was governed, it is clear from his work that this is not what he had in mind. A wide reader of fiction and poetry, a lover of good drama, he demonstrated a conventional taste in these areas; and he confined his own creative activity to one poem (his Harvard class ode) and to musical composition. For a close parallel to what he meant by a literary career we need to turn to men like Emerson and Carlyle and, to some extent perhaps, to Thoreau. In the final analysis, John Fiske should not be evaluated as a scientist or philosopher, possibly not even as a historian, but as a lecturer and, in this carefully defined sense, as a man of letters.

In many respects, Fiske was close to the Transcendentalists in the kind of career he envisioned, if not entirely in the message which he offered. There is in him a strong tendency toward the teacher or preacher; it might be more accurate to say the poet-prophet, the seer, the poet-legislator of Shelley. The dream was to bring through letters the gospel of evolution to the world—to reconcile science and religion for mankind. Concretely, this desire leads in a broader sense to a sweeping analysis of the universe and to an almost chauvinistic conclusion that the Anglo-American race is the epitome of evolution, the promise for the future. Unhappy as both men might have been to be compared, Fiske and Walt Whitman played similar roles in the history of American culture.

In the quiet of Middletown, Fiske thoughtfully assessed his intellectual stock-in-trade and turned his attention quite naturally to the philosophy of history as interpreted through the doctrine of evolution. The aim, it would seem, would be to show how this philosophical point of view had operated down through the ages and what a wonderful clear light it would throw on the history of man. Interestingly enough, and again quite naturally, his first results, like those of Henry and Brooks Adams, developed into two essays about the "Laws of History." Shooting for a star, he sent them off to George Henry Lewes, editor of the *Fortnightly Review,* who promptly accepted both, thus adding to the "English success" which John felt had impressed his stepfather.

Two pertinent quotations show clearly Fiske's feeling about these laws. In notes for the essays he wrote: "But could we attain to a knowledge commensurate with the facts—could we reach the hidden depths, where according to Dante, the story of Nature scattered over the universe in truant leaves, is lying firmly bound in a mystic volume, we should find therein no traces of hazard or incongruity."[30] We are reminded directly of Hawthorne's observations about the perfection of nature as seen through a microscope as compared with the imperfections of the works of man and the wonderful passage near the end of Thoreau's *Walden* in which he describes finding a common form in the spring sand bank, vegetation, and the internal organs of man and animal. Each in his own way emphasizes the underlying perfect unity of nature when even dimly perceived by our limited abilities. Fiske added: "Doubtless to many persons the views here maintained may seem all but atheistical. They are precisely the reverse. Our choice is no longer between an intelligent cause and none at all. It lies between a limited cause and one that is without limit."[31] Typically, Fiske derived his laws from the field of science and proceeded to support them with a reference from a great poet. The note of the mystic echoes through his thinking from first to last; for, as he wrote about Jonathan Edwards, "Now in the mind of Jonathan Edwards there is a vein of mysticism as unmistakable as that in the mind of William Penn. Such mysticism may be found in minds of medium capacity, but in minds of the highest type I believe it is rarely absent. A mind which has plunged deeply into the secrets of nature without exhibiting such a vein of mysticism is, I believe, a mind sterilized and cut off in one direction from access to the truth."[32]

Although the first of these essays was soon published and attracted wide attention, little else that was concrete came from these months in his grandmother's home. As usual, Fiske could report to his friends a voluminous amount of reading and study; there is a good deal of communication with Spencer, primarily on the question of where men of their views can find a publication outlet; and, toward the end, there came the essay "University Reform." This last was prepared as a direct result of a request from Cambridge; for at Harvard the long-simmering pot had come to a boil.

III   A New Harvard

By a legislative act of 1865 the Commonwealth of Massachusetts withdrew from direct connection with the Harvard Board of Overseers so that, from Commencement Day in 1866, all members of the board were to be elected by the alumni. The younger generation was beginning to assume control. On this day, as orator, the Reverend Frederic Hedge (class of 1828) delivered a ringing challenge for a new era. John Fiske had come up from Middletown to receive his master's degree; and, after the ceremonies, Professor Gurney, long a proponent of the modern view, suggested that Fiske was the proper man to present the plan of needed changes in an essay. John Spencer Clark, one of the publishers of the *Atlantic Monthly*, seconded the motion with the assurance that editor James T. Fields would be delighted to receive such an essay. So "University Reform" was written and appeared in the *Atlantic* in April, 1867.

Fiske did his job well: the article is carefully designed not to alarm too greatly those who did not approve of the idea of reform and, at the same time, to enlist the support of the new party. While he could not hope to deal with the subject without arousing some opposition, he kept it to a minimum by his opening announcement that reform was not revolution. He clearly recognized that a New England college founded in a Puritan environment and originally for training ministers was not a German university and should not be. Certainly, the restrictions on undergraduate freedom needed modification as soon as possible, but these were not to be swept away peremptorily: "The New England mind, which tolerates Maine liquor laws and sabbatarian ordinances and protective tariffs, would not regard with favour such a revolutionary measure. So much liberty would bear an uncanny resemblance to license—a resemblance which, we freely admit, might not at first be wholly imaginary."[33]

Reform should be made by first determining the aims and purposes of a university and then making adjustments all along the line to meet those aims: "The whole duty of a university toward those who are sheltered within its walls may be concisely summed up in two propositions. It consists, first, in stimulating the mental faculties of each student to varied and harmonious activity,—in supplying every available instrument for sharpening the perceptive powers, strengthening the judgment, and adding precision and accuracy to the imagination; secondly, in providing for all those students who desire it a means of acquiring a thorough elementary knowledge of any given branch of science, art, or literature. In a word, to teach the student how to think for himself, and then to give him the material to exercise his thought upon,—this is the whole duty of a university."[34]

To achieve these goals, a well-balanced curriculum with both mathematics and the sciences and the classical studies must be developed. For all of his interest in science, John Fiske was too well aware of the values of the older classics to cast them aside. Much of the essay is painstakingly devoted to problems which college faculties still have under discussion: methods of teaching, specialization and vocational training, academic penalties for nonacademic sins, and the balance between required courses and electives. Finally, he proposes a postgraduate course: "Our literature cannot hope to compete with that of other countries, so long as our young men of literary taste and ability have no choice but to embark in an active profession or engage in mercantile employments. . . . A system of post-graduate instruction is, we repeat, the great need of both the university and of the country. Literature, science, and high scholarship have never prospered where they have not been recognized as legitimate special pursuits."[35]

This program was, indeed, sound and sensible. It reveals a good deal about John Fiske in its very solidity: there was nothing bold or daring about it. With no intention of implying any criticism of the judgments pronounced by Fiske, we can observe how thoroughly John Fiske's idea of a university complemented John Fiske the individual. That his idea also spoke very accurately about what Harvard needed is evidenced from several sources: the commencement speech of the Reverend Hedge, the reforms instituted by the new president, and chapters from the biographies of Fiske's Harvard contemporaries like Oliver Wendell Holmes, Jr.

Now openly and publicly aligned with the reform movement and recognized as one of its leading voices, Fiske was becoming excited about the possibilities for Harvard and for himself. At long last he saw the chance of a position in the academic world; and in March, 1867, he moved joyfully back to Cambridge to be on the spot. Opposition among the powers was far from dead, but approval of his article by such people as Longfellow, Lowell, Gurney, and Gray indicated that Fiske had powerful support at the university. But it was some two years later, after the election of Charles W. Eliot to the Harvard presidency, that these hopes bore fruit. And it was a long time before Eliot managed to develop the graduate program that Fiske had called for.

Considering his own boyhood talent and his mother's artistic ability, it is a little odd that Fiske never ventured into art criticism. A possible reason for lack of confidence is indirectly suggested in an essay on Hippolyte Taine in which Fiske blames Puritanism for hindering the growth of art appreciation in England and America: "The Puritan movement, in proportion to its success, was nearly as destructive to art in the West, as Mohammedanism had long before been in the East. In its intense and one-sided regard for morality, Puritanism not only relegated the love of beauty to an inferior place, but condemned and spat upon it.... Hence the bewildered ignorant way in which we ordinarily contemplate pictures and statues. For two centuries we have been removed from an artistic environment, and consequently can with difficulty enter into the feelings of those who have all this time been nurtured in love for art, and believe in art for its own sake."[36]

Fiske pays complete tribute to Puritan virtues and to the excellent foundation they provided for Anglo-American character, but he laments that this particular aspect has led to a still-felt narrow incompleteness. The concluding remark comes close to summarizing his own taste: "It will be a long time before we cease to regard pictures and statues as a higher species of upholstery."[37] But even in music, where his training and knowledge were sufficient for him to perform and to write criticism, he stayed generally solidly with Mozart, Beethoven, and the opera. It is perhaps not surprising that a Victorian should focus his musical esthetic largely in an emotional range, but we are a bit startled to find the same adjectives applied to Beethoven and to John Knowles Paine—the loyalty of a friend can indeed be deaf.

In May, 1867, the first son, Harold Brooks Fiske, was born. Since Abby was not downstairs to supervise the household, there was some confusion with the cook. But this difficulty was minor; John was too busy supervising the garden and the croquet-ground to be long upset by matters inside the house. Far more important, late that summer he met William Dean Howells, a neighbor who was to become a lifelong friend.

The fall and winter contained a number of visits to New York, where Fiske saw a good deal of Manton Marble of the New York *World* apparently for the purpose of balancing out the possibilities of two sources of income: more regular writing assignments and an established academic career. On the one hand, he was doing a great amount of writing for Marble and hoping for even greater opportunities. On the other hand, Marble was using his influence to get Fiske an offer of a professorship at the newly established Cornell University. Fiske's own interest was strongly directed toward writing. The dickering over the academic appointment went on for several years; in the end, it developed into a visiting lectureship or an informal invitation to include the university whenever his lectures took him near Ithaca. Fiske seems to have gone through the motions of showing interest mainly through a sense of duty. Writing to his wife, he reported, "I kept my appointment with White. I got from him pretty thorough information about Cornell University and about Ithaca. What I have heard of it and seen of him, while it is all pleasant enough, does not make my mouth water after the place any more than before."[38] There may have been in all of this a mildly Machiavellian scheming to make Harvard move with a counteroffer. But surely motives of love and duty far outweighed any thoughts of shrewd political maneuvering: duty, in that he could ill afford to ignore opportunities for regular income—possible jobs had at least to be investigated; love, in that Cambridge was his mecca, and living away from here or Petersham was, in the long run, unthinkable.

For the most part, Fiske's literary activities in the late 1860's consisted of innumerable book reviews on a wide range of subjects for the *World* and for such notable periodicals as the *North American Review, Atlantic Monthly,* and *Christian Examiner.* In his position as book reviewer Fiske came upon a volume by James Parton, *Smoking and Drinking,* in which the contention was that future man would abandon both vices. At first, this subject seems a rather superficial one for the attention of a potential great scholar. But Parton's book reflected the temperance aspect of the reform movement, and Fiske felt that organized reform interfered with the slow working out of the evolutionary law of social progress. Furthermore, it touched closely on two of his dearly loved indulgences—his pipe and his beer. Regarding the topic as a scientific subject, John brought his heavy artillery to bear and produced his first book, *Tobacco and Alcohol: It Does Pay to Smoke—The Coming Man Will Drink Wine.* His argument was to remove the whole question from the social reformers and to place it where he felt it belonged, with the medical doctors; thus he marshaled quotations in seven languages from books on physiology and pathology to prove that Parton was wrong.

Although Fiske himself seems to have had a sound evaluation of what he had done—"I can't see that my 'Tobacco and Alcohol' is a 'wonderful mosaic of learning,' or that there is anything very wonderful about it, although it appears to me to be satisfactory and sensible"[39]—nevertheless, it was taken seriously and rated reviews by E. L. Godkin and Charles W. Eliot. In the light of modern cancer research, it is ironic to note that his book received many commendations from the medical profession. Yet it is logical that physicians would tend to agree that this was a medical rather than a moral question. On another level, there was a moral question involved; the attack had been launched as much because of Parton himself as his subject: "According to my notions, a man who tries to instruct the public on a subject which he has never taken the pains to study is more or less of an impostor. And it was because I regarded Parton as something of an impostor—not by any means merely because I disagreed with him—that I treated him so contemptuously in my book. If I had supposed him to be a genuine seeker after truth, I should have written in a very different tone of course."[40]

The Fiskes were great concert and theatergoers and personally acquainted with such theater "greats" as Sir Henry Irving. Attending a series of tragedies starring Edwin Booth and Madame Janauschek, John was deeply moved: she was "the greatest actress since Mrs. Siddons" and completely superb as Lady Macbeth. "The sleep-walking and 'Out damned spot' and the wringing of the hands were unequalled by anything I have seen her do before."[41] Earlier in the year Charles Dickens had been in Boston to give readings from his works. John told his mother, "Last week we heard Dickens read 'Little Dombey' and 'The Trial.' Early in March when we tried to get tickets to hear him I stood four hours freezing in the cold wind and then gave it up."[42] He adds no record of his response to the performance when he finally got there. Knowing his great fondness for Dickens' novels, we wonder why he was able to resist reporting reactions and why he made no attempt to meet the great man.

The resignation of Harvard's President Hill in September, 1868, brought further opportunity for the reformers to show their strength. In the debate about a successor, it soon became clear that the choice was to be between the traditional pattern and the new one—between a clergyman and a professional educator. This division soon focused on the two candidates, the Reverend Andrew Peabody (interim president) and Professor Ephraim Gurney. Since reforms had already been instituted, the selection of the new president would essentially indicate the speed and extent to which change would continue. To present the case for the new party, Fiske was asked by Lowell and E. L. Godkin of the New York *Nation* to write an article summarizing the situation; but the intention was to kill the candidacy of Peabody and promote that of Gurney. The article, appearing in the December, 1868, issue, effectively argued against the tradition: "What we do not want is a mere business man, a fossil man, an ultra-radical man or a clergyman."[43] At the same time, it pointed to an even greater reformer than Gurney. Whether Fiske's editorial can truly be said to have been the decisive factor cannot now be determined, but unquestionably it set forth lucidly and simply the position of the younger faction.

Possibly, in his zeal, he overstated his case; for politically he had much to gain were his friend Gurney to be appointed. There followed two essays by Charles W. Eliot—professor at Massachusetts Institute of Technology, former Harvard instructor and graduate of the class of 1853—in the *Atlantic,* one in February and one in March, both bearing the title, "The New Education —Its Organization." The ideas presented echoed so well the kind of man that Fiske's article had described that Eliot was shortly (though not without strong opposition) chosen the new president of Harvard.

Eliot was, in fact, an excellent choice. Whether through inertia or opposition, the new spirit of science had not penetrated education; the very thing which Fiske had originally sought at Harvard was now to be developed with his assistance. During Fiske's own college years, Eliot had been on the Harvard faculty—had, moreover, before Fiske's coming, worked behind the scenes on President Walker to develop the new science programs and to treat college students as men.

In the same period, John rejected an offer of editorship of

a free-trade journal in New York at a salary of six thousand dollars a year. Ostensibly, he was absorbed in planning a volume on education and in bringing together his ideas on the relationships between language and evolution; but, in fact, he was gambling on Harvard College. This time the rewards were concrete. President Eliot moved fast and even before his inauguration had drawn up a plan for a series of seven lecture courses on philosophy. Eliot's purpose was twofold: he hoped that the series might be a basis for developing a solid post-graduate course; and, by his choice of lecturers, he announced that all views should be heard—both traditional and new. The first course was to be "The Natural History of the Intellect," and the lecturer was to be Ralph Waldo Emerson; the second, "The Positive Philosophy," and the lecturer John Fiske. Through the new president, alma mater was recalling her wayward children. Their philosophies may have caused her to shudder, but at least in part they were forgiven, and their voices were to be heard in university halls. From his letter to his mother, Fiske makes it clear that his acceptance was partly in this spirit: he saw the invitation as recompense for the near expulsion of only eight years before for promulgating these same ideas. His other reason is an acute awareness of the honor and prestige that might forward his career. Eliot's other appointments indicated that his own leaning was toward the men with the new scientific and skeptical attitude: among them were Gurney, dean of faculty; Henry Adams, assistant professor of history; and Oliver Wendell Holmes, Jr., lecturer in the law school.

Outside the walls of Harvard, Fiske's lectures ordinarily would not have created a stir; they did not in themselves draw vast audiences. However through Youmans' efforts, it was arranged that Fiske's lectures were to appear unabridged in the New York *World*. (With Eliot's knowledge or approval?) Needless to say, the first lecture was introduced with a bit of journalistic purple, including the elevation of the author to "Professor Fiske."

The immediate response was an attack from the religious groups on "Harvard's raid on religion." The old enemy opened fire on Fiske, President Eliot, and the *World*. Eliot and Gurney were privately annoyed; this might easily damage the entire new program; but they were not frightened off. Operating on the adage that the best defense is a strong offense, Eliot immediately commended Fiske on the lectures and requested their repetition the following year, with an additional course focused on the philosophy of evolution from the English point of view. These two courses gave Fiske the opportunity to develop the ideas which later became a major book, *The Outlines of Cosmic Philosophy,* and the foundation of his reputation as a philosopher. It is not too great an exaggeration to suggest that all the rest of his philosophical writing and lecturing was in large part an extension of that book. Fiske himself, at least for many years, considered it his greatest contribution.

But the old order was not dead. The proponents of science might claim they had no true quarrel with religion, and John Fiske might insist that he had no quarrel with God—and, indeed, he had not—but the orthodox church had a quarrel with John Fiske, and the church still held some power on the Harvard Board. However the clergy might protest against Fiske's Spencerian philosophy, it was really his rejection of the divine inspiration of the Bible that brought charges of atheism. In January, 1870, when Professor Gurney was appointed dean, Eliot had nominated Fiske to occupy Gurney's chair as an acting professor of history for the spring term. Only a very strong action by Eliot and board members James Freeman Clarke and Edward Everett Hale brought through the appointment by a bare majority; the old charges of atheism might have been fatal had Clarke not taken the trouble to read Fiske's lectures as they had appeared in the New York *World.* The bitter resistance of the board to even this temporary appointment made it evident that John Fiske could not count on joining the faculty—at least not for a long time to come. It was thus that Eliot and Gurney appealed to Henry Adams to fill the vacancy in the department of history. Though the theologians thereby closed one door firmly for the immediate future, the official appointments which they had permitted seemed to be opening new doors.

One of these doors was the possibility of publication, which Fiske had so thoroughly discussed with Spencer that the suggestion was made that Fiske might bring out simultaneous English and American editions because of the problems of international copyright, that they debated about the title, and that they discussed things to be done "when you come to England." Another door that was opened was the possibility of extensive

lecturing. First came an invitation to repeat the entire Harvard
course in Milwaukee, sponsored by John's old friend, the Reverend Dudley. This invitation was followed by a request to
repeat the series in Boston in the winter of 1872; and, in the
midst of all this lecturing, Harvard in May, 1872, offered Fiske
an appointment as assistant librarian, a post which Fiske had
not sought but was most happy to accept. Eliot was a determined
man; and, from his later actions, we might conjecture that he
was consciously trying to provide Fiske with security yet leave
him free to work. The new voices would be heard.

Eliot had indicated his position earlier when reporting on his
disappointment at the failure to obtain for Fiske an invitation to
the Lowell Institute: "I am sorry for this obstacle to your progress; but I beg you not to be discouraged, and not to abandon
faith in the force of scholarship, and sincerity, and in the real
and ultimate liberality of this community."[44]

However indirect a bearing such things may have in analyzing
Fiske as a writer, occasional sketches of domestic life are
essential to a portrait of Fiske the man. His frank and even
sentimental attachment to family life, typically Victorian, fills
pages of his letters with detailed accounts of home, garden,
and children. The births of Ralph Browning Fiske in 1870 and
of Ethel in 1872 brought the total to five—no wonder that a
man with champagne tastes had to keep an eye on the family
budget. And he had become something of a gourmet, as his
size was beginning to show. But reports of visits to the circus
and to Barnum museums bulk larger than the problems of
making both ends meet; Fiske took as keen a delight in such
simple pleasures as did his children. During the middle years
of his life a good portion of these family sketches come from
Petersham and are summer idylls. The scenes of picnics, rambles
through the woods, and other country excursions which run
through the letters from this time on are like a collection of
Currier and Ives prints. Fiske's interest in nature might occasionally focus on the scientific, especially with some botanizing;
but on the whole, its tone is pastoral and domestic. A poem
like *Snowbound* comes closer to his kind of appreciation than
Walden would.

On a more sophisticated level, there were dinners at Del-
monico's when he visited his parents in New York, a dinner

party given by John Hay, and a literary dinner in Fiske's honor given by the publisher William Appleton. The guest list included such notables as George Ripley and William Cullen Bryant. The Fiskes were also present at the famous party given by the Howells for Bret Harte. Fiske has no comment to make on Harte but evidently enjoyed himself hugely: "Fields, Longfellow, Lowell, Thomas Bailey Aldrich, Henry James, Sedgwick ... and many others were there, so many we knocked elbows. Everyone wore his best bib and tucker, the house is well arranged for entertaining, and the supper was delicious—provided by the caterer Smith. Mrs. Howells was very pretty and charming; vivacious and amusing as always. We were among the last to leave shortly before midnight."[45]

Early in 1873 Fiske's first real book, *Myths and Mythmakers*, was published. In a small way, this delightful little book is a parallel in all of its characteristics to all of the rest of the books which John Fiske was to write. Its admitted approach is to synthesize; in the preface, Fiske acknowledges that he has contributed nothing original but has freely used Jacob Grimm, Max Müller, Adalbert Kuhn, Michel Bréal, Sir George Dasent, and Edward Taylor. On a second level, he has also synthesized by collecting and interweaving previously published essays of his own. Its purpose, which reflects his role of teacher, is to present scholarly materials in such a way as to arouse general interest. (The Victorian was not worried about the problem of cheapening culture by offering it to the people!)

Its theme, of course, is evolution: through comparative philology Fiske traces the evolution of various myths back to sources which in general indicate prescientific attempts to explain nature: "The religious myths of antiquity and the fireside legends of ancient and modern times have their common root in the mental habits of primeval humanity. They are the earliest recorded utterances of men concerning the visible phenomena of the world into which they were born."[46] He will have none of the sophisticated theory that myths were originally designed as allegory: "Primitive men had no profound science to perpetuate by means of allegory, nor were they such sorry pedants as to talk in riddles when plain language would serve their purpose. Their minds, we may be sure, worked like our own, and when they spoke of the far-darting sun-god, they

meant just what they said, save that where we propound a
scientific theorem, they constructed a myth."[47] It may be a
long jump, for example, from William Tell to primitive explanations of the sun's path or the lightning bolt; but Fiske's argument
makes this convincing. First he cites historical record to prove
that the story of Tell was not an actual event; then he demonstrates its origin through a number of parallel stories, all of
which he traces back to related explanations of natural
phenomena.

Stemming from his early training with Mr. Colton, one of
Fiske's earliest scholarly achievements was in the area of
philology; and he naturally resorts to it whenever possible. It
becomes a major tool in his first book, as part of his proof of
the way in which simple explanations of the occurrences in
nature evolved into legend, allegory, and religious patterns.
And two interesting side notes might be mentioned here: first,
while Fiske certainly operates in a scholarly and scientific
manner, there is still an echo of the intuitive concept that all
words originated as concrete things. Second, Fiske's contemporaries might well have been entertained by phenomenological
bases for Greek gods, but they were not equally delighted to
have the process applied to Christianity and the Bible. John
Fiske might follow the "higher criticism" in separating myth
from fact in the Bible—indeed, he might feel that this added
to the dignity of God—but there were those who called this
blasphemy and held it to be additional evidence that the new
science was akin to atheism.

Side by side with Sanskrit phrases, Greek history, and esoteric
learning, *Myths and Mythmakers* contains homely references to
country things in Petersham, Massachusetts, in 1870. While these
may consciously have been included as a means of relating the
scholarly to the popular, they are nevertheless characteristic of
the Romantic following Wordsworth, of the Victorian, and of
the American. Such folksy examples occur, for example, not
only in the writings of men like Benjamin Franklin and John
Woolman but in the writings of Jonathan Edwards. To many
people, the connection between the folk medicine still practiced
and the more academic topics must have been made clearer
by including these concrete and immediate illustrations. And
the reality of sorcery must have been sharpened by the example

of the dousers and their operations in Petersham. This particular passage, incidentally, underlines rather vividly Fiske's way of thinking; for his confidence in evolution and in the continuous enlightenment of man is sometimes a bit naïve: "These men were seeking water with a divining-rod. Here, alive before my eyes, was a superstitious observance which I had supposed long since dead and forgotten by all men except students interested in mythology."[48] More disillusioned after one hundred years, we are more prone to realize that scientific explanations have not eliminated superstition.

However, Fiske's own attempt to use the rod combines a pleasant anecdote with a sharp psychological observation. The divining rod completely refused to work for him, and the explanation of the farm boy was meditative: "Well, you see, your temperament is peculiar; the conditions ain't favorable in your case; there are some people who never can work these things. But there's water below there, for all that, as you'll find if you dig for it; there's nothing like a hazel rod for finding water."[49] Yes, Fiske observes, there are some people who never can make these things work. Their ill-success is commonly ascribed to lack of faith; but, in the majority of cases, it might be more truly referred to the strength of their faith—faith in the constancy of nature and in the adequacy of ordinary human experience as interpreted by science.

Finally, this early book is an excellent example of Fiske's style, which seems to move so lucidly, so swiftly, so smoothly, and with such effective use of concrete illustration through the material that he is presenting that the reader is convinced that he understands. Perhaps the secret is the easy display of wide information if not of broad learning; perhaps it is the prodigious memory that holds innumerable facts and illustrations ready for use; perhaps it is the optimistic confidence on the part of the writer—perhaps all, or none, of these. But we can already see the great talent which Fiske has for making his subject readable and attractive, the foundation for his reputation as a great popularizer (in the best sense); and less fortunately, we can see part of the reason why more solemn scholars have been reluctant to grant him full academic honors. The book was appropriately dedicated to "my dear friend, William Dean

Howells, in remembrance of pleasant evenings spent among werewolves, and trolls, and nixies."

Repeating the philosophy lectures in Boston in the winter of 1873, Fiske attracted wider audiences than he had done a year before—and gained a patron. Mrs. M. A. Edwards, "regarding as very important the religious implications of the philosophy of Evolution" as he had presented it, quietly sent Abby a check for one thousand dollars that John might go to England to consult personally with Spencer, Huxley, Lewes, and others and revise his lectures into the proper form for the proposed book. At the next meeting of the Harvard Corporation, Fiske's position in the library was unanimously confirmed for life; and Eliot secured him a leave of absence for one year beginning in August. And, to clear away remaining financial obstacles, James Brooks offered to assume all of the domestic expenses for the time Fiske was to be away.

The plans that were made with great gusto have more the ring of a young man about to make the grand tour than of a scholar going abroad to arrange for publication. With his usual enthusiasm, Fiske included in his plans only a little less than reasonable time to complete his work in England and, at first, followed this with a great sweep across Europe as far as Constantinople. Little by little this plan was curtailed. A most interesting contrast, characteristic of Fiske, is shown as he works on his travel plans. There is the almost boyish enthusiasm which proposed vast schemes for absorbing the whole continent —this John Fiske took the cosmos for his province; and there is the painstaking detail with which he worked out a complete itinerary with a project for every day of the journey and wrote the whole thing down meticulously—this John Fiske loved facts and details.

In a whirl of activity, he made arrangements to sail August 12 on the *Olympus* for England. Among other things, he completed and mailed the last article for which he was committed the evening before he boarded the ship. Unfortunately, this article attacked Agassiz on the old question of creation by divine fiat— unfortunately, because Agassiz was very ill and died only two months after the article appeared. The circumstances made Fiske appear unjust and unfeeling. In a way, the sailing of that steamer from Boston rounded off a chapter in Fiske's life. Not that it marks any sharp division; rarely does this happen outside of fiction; for there are always continuing threads that interweave and overlap. Nor can we say that magically from this day forward the career that Fiske had dreamed and worked for moved ever upward. But the European experience and the European reputation—or rumors of his European reputation—worked their way. There were later ups and downs, later tacks of direction, but no more false starts.

CHAPTER 3

The Philosopher

I *First Trip Abroad*

WHATEVER method we choose for separating the various strands of a man's life and work is bound to be, to some extent, arbitrary. From the beginning Fiske gave his attention concurrently to the major fields of his interest: philology, philosophy, and history. In the broadest sense, all three were so thoroughly intertwined as to be to a great extent facets of the same subject. Nevertheless, there is a slow shift of emphasis; for a peak in the philosophical writing comes with the publication of *Outlines of Cosmic Philosophy*. After this book, his work in this area is largely concerned with reconciling his scientific position with his religious faith—not a change of position but an almost imperceptible one of focus (and he would never consent to the word "reconcile"). After his return from Europe, Fiske became more and more captivated with the evolutionary interpretation of American history.

Aside from the all-important philosophical work, there are two aspects of his first trip abroad which cannot be overlooked: the impressions of the European landscape and the effect of the social life in which he was involved. Unfortunately, not until some years after his death did Fiske's public gain the opportunity to read of his travels in Europe. It is much to be regretted that he did not publish a book similar to his friend Howells' *Italian Journeys* instead of leaving these impressions recorded only in letters to his family. These letters, posthumously printed, contain some of Fiske's most delightful writing. Released from the need of appearing scholarly, they are fresh and free, with charming impressions of scenery, architecture, fine arts, and important people. While no one could claim for these letters a high degree of profundity, they are nevertheless an enlightening addition to the international literary theme later expounded by Henry James; an interesting comparison to Mark Twain's *Innocents Abroad*; and, above all, a most revealing portrait of the personality of John Fiske.

Fiske's Scotland is tinted with the colors of Sir Walter Scott; his England is largely the world of Dickens; his esthetic reaction to landscape carries a romanticized version of Burke on the sublime; and, with his awareness of history, his whole view of Europe is colored by a strong sense of the past; finally, the entire scene is measured against the norm—or epitome—of Petersham, Massachusetts. This comparison reflects not so much a provincial manner as quite simply the reaction of a man who loves his native soil. Ireland is lovelier than anything he has ever experienced, and the Scottish highlands have a majestic awe that New England cannot match. And, like Hawthorne and Henry James, Fiske recognizes the long influence of man in creating something that America did not have (Matthew Arnold called it "distinction"). But, while his eyes may be lifted up, his soul swept by grandeur, his heart is ever fixed in the Berkshire hills. Nor was he unaware of his predilection: "I don't know that Switzerland is more *sublime* than Scotland, for nothing can excell in sublimity Loch Linnhe, and Glencoe, and the awful moor by the King's House Inn. I don't know that it is more *beautiful* than Italy, meaning by beauty 'what the eye admires.' And I don't know that it is any more *lovely* than Petersham—meaning by lovely what the heart clings to. But for sublimity, beauty, and loveliness *combined,* I say that Switzerland is so far above all other countries that there is no use in saying anything more about it."[1]

We must not draw from this example the impression that his descriptions are sentimental, touristlike "ohs" and "ahs." There is sentiment, perhaps even sentimentality; but, on the whole, Fiske's perceptions are sharper than this. The strongest note of the sentimental comes in response to children and is based on a sense of homesickness justifiable in any father. It is all very well for Fiske to romp with the young Huxleys, to dandle the Trübner children on his knee, and to offer a winsome Italian beggar child a penny for a kiss; but how did Herbert Spencer, for example, really enjoy being exposed to pictures of the col-

60

JOHN FISKE

lective Fiske children tumbling about in a basket wagon? It is just as well that John did not voice the thought which he tells Abby flashed through his mind as he displayed the photograph: "By jove, that wagon-load is worth more than all the *philosophy that ever was concocted*, from Aristotle to Spencer."[2]

And there are striking notes of humor. Fiske finds his oral French completely useless in Paris and reverts to German to make his needs known to a waiter. But in Italy on a visit to a library where English is not spoken, he carries on for hours in French. And his comments on food are those of a gourmet— even a gourmand—though not of the Cordon Bleu variety. Over all runs the basic emotional bias (not unnatural for a nineteenth-century Bostonian) which is fixedly pro-British. The Anglo-American attitude may appear in formal histories as an intellectual theory; essentially, it is not. The letters demonstrate that this trait is an inborn sense of family which he could not have divorced from his thinking if he had wanted to. English cathedrals are superior to those on the Continent; art exhibits in England are more impressive than those in the Louvre; and British cooking—good old beef and ale—cannot be matched in overrated France. As for the people, except for the individuals whom he meets socially, he sees stereotypes; and only the English, Scotch, and Irish are home folks.

Even the natives of the British Isles, cousins though they might be, are praised with qualifications. British speech at first offends his ear—the English sound guttural like Germans. And, on a rainy day in Scotland, he observes: "This is a land where Puritanism still holds sway; which doesn't prevent it from being the most intemperate country on the face of the globe. Asceticism and mental acuteness, drunkenness and thrift, somehow manage to get along together."[3] The Irish, on the other hand, are more delightful than their compatriots who have emigrated. "For I notice that the Paddy at home, if he is in a decent station in life, appears far better than his degenerate brother who comes to America. The Paddy at home has never learned to be democratic and sassy, i.e. he shows a riverance in his manners which greatly becomes him."[4]

Reactions to the English landscape, partly depending, it is true, on variations in mood, were contradictory. On the one hand, "it has all the monotony of a face which is perfect in beauty, without any play of expression." The neatness, order, and symmetry are too well manicured for the American eye; and we are amused at the note of homesickness for American casualness, not to say slovenliness, "you never see old tomato-cans, cuttings of tin, piles of brush, and so on, by the roadside. . . . In short, it is the cleanest, happiest, most smiling landscape conceivable; and the effect of about a hundred miles of it is to weary the eye so that you are glad to look away from it, and read your guide book or the newspaper."[5] On the other hand, a long sweep through the Continent and France in particular, made him long for England with her clean little cottages and ordered country lanes. "No wonder they love nature so much that Taine doesn't quite understand 'em. But *la belle* France is a poor country in comparison."[6] Fiske conceded that the Seine was prettier than the Thames; but—like Whistler—he found the views from Waterloo Bridge magnificent.

The phrase "European landscape" should probably be broadened to "European environment" since it is meant to include a great deal more than natural scenery. At Innesfallen, Fiske describes the magnificent beeches and holly trees, contrasts the deep green of the ivy with the blue of the lake, and is awed by the mountains covered with purple heather; but it takes the addition of human association to bring the "chokes" and tears. "All the long, long past, richly freighted with memories came rushing by me, as I sat listening to the soft dropping of the summer shower on the holly leaves, and to the delicious song of the thrush—at my feet a grave where one of those heroes of Christianity had slept a thousand years."[7]

Fiske's response to works of art is equally compounded of esthetic emotion and sentiment. His taste in architecture, and the principles behind it, would be anathema to Horatio Greenough, Louis Sullivan, or Frank Lloyd Wright. To Fiske, Americans don't know how to design a decent building; and he wonders why, at Harvard, "we don't honestly confess our stupidity, and show some grains of sense by *copying* the Oxford or Cambridge buildings literally!"[8] Closer to his attitude at Innesfallen is a later reaction to two statues; one by Michelangelo; the other, a Greek *Melpomene*: "You would instantly see the incomparable superiority of the Greek. I could have stood there looking at it till now; it brought the tears, not because there was any sentiment in it, in point of sentiment, the superiority was on the side of the *David*. The thing about the *Melpomene* which stirred me so much was simply the incredible beauty of form, the matchless symmetry, the triumph of human genius over marble, which affected me like the purest harmony of Mozart."[9]

Immediately following is a reference to Gotthold Lessing's *Laokoön,* which may account for this unusual preference for form. Yet it must be admitted that Fiske's reaction to sculpture was generally more sophisticated than that toward paintings. With the latter he is rarely moved sufficiently to do more than apply the conventional adjectives, but in Florence a picture by Sacconi evokes a paragraph of description, and this time the focus is more typically on mood. "A thinker tired and overwhelmed with the mystery of the problem of existence," which again moves him to tears and is compared to music. "Something which seemed to say—the riddle is hard but behind the veil is an answer yet."[10] Fiske echoes the tone and interpretations called forth by the Adams memorial in Rock Creek Park.

Esthetically, these are high points and indeed a long way from the young Fiske who chose an engraving because of the historical figures portrayed. More characteristic even now is the habit of associating an English day with a painting by Turner or of describing London fog by quoting verbatim from memory the opening pages of Dickens' *Bleak House.* And he is equally quick to respond emotionally, though not with tears, to Madame Tussaud's wax museum or to a carnival in the great square at Bruges. In spite of being "awfully tired," he visited the fair and stayed until midnight: "It was one of the richest and jolliest sights I have seen in Europe—Dwarfs and Giants, operatic performances, pictures, hobby-horse riding, games, trials of strength, and so on. I went in for everything! Laughing and talking with the people."[11]

Fiske's writing had guaranteed him acquaintances in England long before he sailed. His work in philology provided a basis for a solid friendship with Dr. John Muir in Edinburgh; his articles and lectures on evolution, a warm welcome from Herbert Spencer. Almost from the first he was a kind of favorite uncle in the Huxley household. With each trip abroad, he was invited to more clubs, given more dinners, met more important people, until a backward glance at those whom he knew—some quite intimately—is like a glance at the roll call of the literary-intellectual elite of the day from Sir Charles Lyell to Tennyson and Alma-Tadema.

Among the portrait sketches which Fiske sent back to Abby and his mother, the one of George Eliot is most entertaining. Always he insisted on referring to her as Mrs. Lewes, obviously out of sheer respect for the character of Miss Evans and Mr. Lewes. He informed his mother that his notions about such things were ascetically strict, but in this case he was convinced that they had done the very best they knew and that few were in a position to cast stones at them. Striking a lighter note, he told Abby that he could not agree with George Eliot's description of herself as homely: "She is better looking than George Sand. She isn't a blooming beauty, of course; you don't expect that at fifty-two." On the one hand, he found her "a real, good, honest, genuine, motherly woman with no nonsense about her." On the other, he noted her great intellectual capacity and her wide education: "She has the power of *stating* an argument equal to any man. Equal to any man, do I say? I have never found any man, except Herbert Spencer, who could state a case equal to her." And she was thoroughly cognizant of the Homeric question, apparently having read Homer in Greek; she was able to give Fiske a run for his money in discussing the question. And yet she was completely feminine; he reconciled the intellectual and the domestic in his final sentence: "She didn't talk like a blue-stocking—as if she were aware she had got hold of a big subject —but like a plain woman, who talked of Homer as simply as she would of flat-irons."[12]

Another portrait worthy of recording was sketched after a luncheon date with Darwin; in this word picture Fiske managed to include by contrast the three Englishmen most important to him philosophically as well as personally:

Darwin is the dearest, sweetest, loveliest old Grandpa that ever was. There is no doubt that Spencer is the profoundest thinker of all these men but Darwin impresses me with his strength more than any man I have ever seen. There is a charming kind of quiet strength about everything he does. He is not burning and eager like Huxley. He has a mild blue eye and his manner is full of repose. He is the gentlest of gentle old fellows. None of these men seem to know how

great they are; but Darwin is one of the most truly modest men I
ever saw, the combination of power and quiet modesty in him is
more impressive than I can describe.... And what is so delightful
to see as that perfect frankness and guileless simplicity of manner
which comes from a man having devoted his whole life to some
great idea, without a thought of self and without ever having become
"a man of the world"?[13]

Such delightful associations meant much to John Fiske, who
loved good society and good living. But beyond the personal
significance is also the fact the lionizing in London did much
to make Fiske a more attractive lecturer and writer to those
back home.

Not all of his time in Europe was spent, however, in touring
and in socializing. He took lodgings in London and worked in
his usual manner, often for long hours a day, preparing the
manuscript for his book. The eighteen original Harvard lectures
of 1869 had been expanded and modified to thirty-five lectures
in 1871; and these were now revised into thirty-nine chapters
of the *Outlines of Cosmic Philosophy*. Somewhat after his return
to the states, the book was published simultaneously by Macmillan in England and by Osgood in America. To determine how
completely those two volumes are a parallel of the ideas of Herbert Spencer would require a detailed comparative analysis
scarcely worth the time and effort. In the first place, Fiske himself made no claim, except for one small bit, to original thought.
The whole pattern of the book constantly reiterates its avowed
purpose; to set forth as clearly as possible the history of the
English school, to set forth its principles as he understood them,
to separate the English carefully from Auguste Comte and posi-
tivism, and to present the implications and values of his philosophy.

In the second place, Fiske gives in his preface a complete
account, citing chapter and verse, of the places where he has
followed and those where he has departed from Spencer. However much he may have confined himself in general to explicating
Spencer, the focus was entirely Fiske: in the final analysis,
this work was to be the definitive one reconciling science and
religion; it was to assure his readers that because of, not in spite
of, evolution, God *is* in His heaven and all's right with the world.
Whatever disappointments may have arisen when scholarly

critics found it necessary to underline that Fiske could not present any claims as an original philosopher, it must be emphasized that he did not seriously make such claims. His own feeling was that originality had its place but should not be the major criterion for judging excellence. This fondness for originality "led the French Academy of Sciences some thirty years ago to elect for a new member some Scandinavian naturalist, whose name I forget, instead of Charles Darwin, inasmuch as the former had described three or four new bugs while the latter was only a constructor of theories."[14]

That many people in Fiske's own day, nevertheless, accorded him the position of original philosopher and that he may well have slipped into playing the role cannot be denied. However, in his printed works, John Fiske almost invariably takes the position of critical historian of philosophic thought, of synthesizer, and of interpreter. Or, to put it another way, his books might be called his sermons and the Spencerian philosophy his text. If all these connotations are included in the definition, we must concur in the twentieth-century judgment that the true role of John Fiske was that of popularizer.

Though for the most part, at least outwardly, heartily approving, Spencer had his reservations. He commended, and later cited, but never made any real use of the one original bit that Fiske included—his theory about the relatively long infancy of the human being. Spencer and Fiske came near to quarreling over the title, Spencer preferring "Synthetic" to "Cosmic." A compromise was finally reached when Spencer agreed to accept the title if the preface would contain a statement setting forth the fact that it was used without his concurrence. In print Fiske fulfilled the request rather gracefully by concluding his prefatory explanation with the statement that, as far as he knew, "the question at issue between us is purely a question of nomenclature, and is not implicated with any essential difference of opinions as to the character and position of the system of thought to which the nomenclature is applied."

But, in a private letter to Abby, he suggested that Spencer simply could not bear to have another person name his "bantling" and stated flatly that he had no intention of backing down; the first volume, as a matter of fact, was ready for press, and he included a specimen page for her to see. What Fiske failed to realize was the fact that this difference reflected Spencer's indifference to the religious implications which Fiske found so important—which, in the long run, were the dramatic climax, the excuse for being of the entire philosophy. It was not encumbent on Herbert Spencer as it was on Fiske to refute the charges of infidel and atheism which had been made so long before in Middletown; and both for his personal comfort and for his public image, this was the crusade upon which John Fiske had embarked.

Without attempting to summarize the entire work, it is worthwhile to focus upon some of the ideas and characteristics involved. The basic pedagogical, not to say pedantic, pattern is not unlike that used in his early essay on Buckle, though Fiske learned to use it less stiffly and mechanically. The scientific method, as John Fiske defined it, was based on verification; but, for the most part, this verification was more through logic than by means of laboratory testing. When applied with a heavy hand, as it sometimes was, this method echoed James Fenimore Cooper's good Dr. Battius, who so thoroughly irritated Natty Bumpo in *The Prairie*.

Fortunately for the reader, Fiske more often erred in the direction of homely language and common-sense explanations. Like the pattern and style, the ideas sometimes echo the early essay and help to show Fiske's basic assumptions, while those ideas which are modified demonstrate his path of growth and change. And it is interesting to note that the emphasis on religion increased from the 1869 lectures which gave one brief consideration in seventeen lectures to religion; the published work gave the question six chapters. This measure, it should be pointed out, is only a matter of direct consideration: religious implications are a running undercurrent from first to last.

Basic to Fiske's argument in the *Outlines* are his insistence on the relativity of knowledge and his definitions of science and philosophy. All knowledge, he says, is relative: knowledge can be gained only through experience. We cannot know, for instance, the actual objects of the natural world, except through the impressions of those objects as presented to us through our consciousness. Thus, the world around us is immediately divided into the knowable and the unknowable: those things which have come within human experience, and those which have not. Science is then defined as a collective term for those branches such as astronomy, biology, geology, psychology—those separate areas in which the known can be verified, expanded, classified. In short, the role of science is to explore and test experience in the attempt to extend the frontiers of knowledge until they reach the point beyond which the mind of man cannot go.

With this objective in mind, it is not surprising to find Fiske stating that science is, after all, but a "higher development of the common information of average minds," that "the process gone through, and the results obtained from the process, are not generically different in scientific and ordinary thinking."[15] Philosophy, the capstone of science, when stripped of all metaphysical aspects (because metaphysics postulates unverifiable hypotheses about the unknowable), finds itself faced with a task similar to that of science in classifying phenomena: "The difference between philosophy and science, like the difference between science and common knowledge, is a difference in degree only. But the distinction is, nevertheless, a broad one." And the difference, most simply stated, is that science "can deal only with particular orders of phenomena; gravitative, or thermal, or chemical, or vital, or psychical, or social phenomena." But "the universe of phenomena is an organic whole," and it is only when truths respecting these classes of phenomena "come to be regarded as corollaries of some universal truth—some truth common to all these orders of phenomena" that we have a philosophy. "While science, in its highest development, is an aggregate of general doctrines, philosophy, in its highest development, must be a Synthesis of all general doctrines into a universal doctrine."[16]

The important thing to note is that these definitions carefully confine both science and philosophy to a study of that which is knowable. Quite beyond their scope lies the Absolute, infinite, eternal God. Thus Cosmism rules out from the beginning any conflict between science and religion. For the cosmic philosophy affirms that the religious sentiment must find satisfaction in the future, as it has in the past, in the recognition of a Power which is beyond humanity and upon which humanity depends. Neither science nor philosophy can deny or define that Power—it remains Unknowable. However, the doctrine of evolution asserts, "as the ultimate truth of science, as the truth upon which the whole structure of human knowledge philosophically rests," the existence of this Power.[17] Since the existence of God is the fundamental postulate upon which Cosmism bases its synthesis or scientific truths, evolutionary science actually has strengthened religion and by its very nature cannot possibly be atheistical. Such a sweeping summary of Fiske's thought is admittedly distorted and generalized; yet it does, I trust, catch the broad outlines against which to set forth more specific aspects of the philosophy.

Again, at the risk of oversimplification, the relation of evolution to this reasoning can be succinctly stated: the law of evolution is one, in fact the very first, of the universal truths "common to all these orders of phenomena" to be discovered. "The law of evolution is the first generalization concerning the concrete universe as a whole, which has been framed in conscious conformity to the rigorous requirements of the objective method, and which has therefore served to realize the prophetic dream of Bacon, by presenting Philosophy as an organism of which the various sciences are members."[18] An explanation such as this one instantly makes clear two points about John Fiske: first, it is the basis on which his interpretation of history will later be based; for in turning to history, he set himself the task of correcting and viewing it scientifically (that is, against the law of evolution) as he hoped others would examine other areas of knowledge. Second, by applying the law of evolution, he found himself correcting the metaphysics and mythology associated with religion, and he thus exposed himself to charges of atheism and infidelism despite all of his carefully reasoned proofs that Cosmism scientifically affirmed the existence of God.

For Fiske, the law of evolution swept aside forever any concept of special creation. By accepting the concept of a slow, natural process of adjustment between organisms and environment, he freed God from anthropomorphic qualities; "while the universe is the manifestation of Deity, Deity is something more than the universe." For John Fiske, this was an exalted kind of Deity, restored to such abstractions as Absolute, infinite, eternal, and unknowable. He could not see the argument of those who regarded this view as relegating God to the position of a remote first cause—a position somehow too impersonal, vague, or abstract

for the emotional needs of many people. Nor does Fiske seem
to be aware that his is, in many respects, the argument, in
contemporary dress, by means of which Emerson and Parker
had distressed the clergy only a generation before.

Applying generally the law of evolution meant that it was
not to be confined to biology or to mere physical development:
social and psychological change was subject to the same law,
moving in its slow, inexorable way. It is a historical fact that
such a view led many to one form or another of determinism,
but Fiske saw only progress. He spends many pages in a rather
complicated argument designed to set aside the contention that
the causation theory, when applied to human history, reduces
man to "a mere link in the chain of causation, a mere grain in
the mass of being." Rather successfully, Fiske demonstrates that
chance and causation are mutually exclusive since the latter
operates by immutable law. But, when he tangles with the
question of the freedom of the will, he manages to present in
scientific or psychological terminology the same sort of argument
which made Oedipus a free agent but still subject to his destiny
—the same sort of argument that permitted Calvinists free will
and predestination. What free will comes to for Fiske is a kind
of liberty under law.

As for the possibility of pessimism, an inevitable descent to
destruction, the idea apparently never even occurs to Fiske.
Assuming that evolution is moral, he says calmly that "the
causationist, believing that volition invariably follows the stronger
motive, endeavors to increase the relative strength of all those
emotions whose outcome is virtuous and upright conduct, while
he strives to weaken those feelings whose tendency is toward
base and ignoble conduct."[19] Presumably, the process itself acts
upon similar principle: evolution strengthened all forms which
lead to progress. In the end of the chapter, he apologizes for
having spent twenty-six pages on such questions as freedom of
the will; for "to many this chapter will no doubt seem like an
elaborate attempt to prove the truth of the multiplication table."[20]
Regretfully, there were many to whom it was the vital question,
and John Fiske's answer was the kind which serves only to
confirm believers. Somewhat later in his life he returned to
this argument with a keener awareness of where the objections

lay; nevertheless, in facing it again, he fell back on belief and faith rather than on science.

Cosmic philosophy maintains that to evolve is to move to a higher state. While Fiske nowhere spells out a definition of the word *progress,* it is always clear from illustration and description that the word carries its traditional meaning of betterment or improvement to the point where the organism (man, for example) comes to a perfect balance with the environment. That this implies a future Golden Age is clearly stated: "It is with reason that the modern mind sees its Golden Age in the distant future, as the ancient mind saw it in the forgotten past." But, like the Christian heaven, Fiske warns, this age lies far ahead along a path of toil and sorrow: "the goal is yet far off, and ... many a weary league must be traversed before we can attain it. Meanwhile, grinding misery is the lot of many, regret and disappointment the portion of all."[21] There is no cause for despair but for quiet resignation and gratefulness that pain and evil exist as correctives, for pain is but the signal that a wrong act has been committed (an act against the environment). Beyond the level of the physical, Fiske defines "survival of the fittest" as survival of those most in tune with the environment.

In all of the involved and elaborate working out of the philosophy, Fiske claims but one idea as wholly original with him: his suggestion that the prolonged infancy of the human child has been the cause of man's moving from savagery to civilization. Civilization could not begin to develop until the law of progress went into operation. In order for this to happen, it was essential for mankind to move from mere gregariousness to what he calls "sociality"—from a crude kind of clan loyalty to a more refined awareness of the need for the submission of the individual for the good of the community. Only when the individual feels sympathy and cooperation strongly enough to sacrifice his own needs for those of others can the movement toward civilization begin. The long infancy of the human child slowly brought into being a more and more prolonged family life; and, in caring for the dependent child, the parents ever so slowly developed these necessary qualities.

At least one other consideration is needed if the argument is to make sense; as it stands, we might well ask why there needed to be any delay. Fiske maintains that the infancy of any being is "the period during which the nerve connections and correlative ideal associations necessary for self-maintenance are becoming permanently established." And the period becomes longer and longer as the intelligence increases in complexity. Thus many forms of life are born with complete capacity; there is, so to speak, no infancy at all. With humans, increasing intelligence continuously lengthened the period until, at some non-definable point along the way, the prolonged infancy awoke sparks of altruism. This point, remote and undiscoverable as it is, nevertheless marks the birth of civilized man. All of which is fine to this point and can be verified or denied by comparative anatomy; but Fiske goes on to insist that the period of infancy is not only longer among men than among the higher animals, but longer among civilized men than among savages, until he reaches the observation that, "Indeed, among the educated classes of civilized society, its average duration may be said to be rather more than a quarter of a century, since during all this time those who are to live by brainwork are simply acquiring the capacity to do so, and are usually supported upon the products of parental labor."[22] The main point is clear enough: somewhere the slowly increasing period of infant dependence held the parents together long enough for the birth, however faint, of family feeling—and, from that point on, man had crossed the bridge from animality to humanity.

Such a brief sampling of the *Outlines of Cosmic Philosophy* does it, perhaps, less than justice in respect to either its scientific or philosophic soundness. It is hoped, however, that even a sample will capture enough to support the statement that Fiske was certainly not a scientist in the modern sense of a painstaking laboratory verifier. Even in his own time, he could not be compared in this respect to Huxley, nor was he a philosopher like Plato; but, ultimately, he was perhaps something of both. His desire to reconcile science and religion was in part a need to reconcile two facets of his own nature—his intellect and his emotions. Throughout the book, the pattern seems scientific and logical; but at crucial points purely subjective jumps are unconsciously made to unchecked conclusions. Despite the training gained in reading contemporary science, neither the Calvinist nor the Transcendentalist environment had quite disappeared. Logical or scientific reasoning was presented in religious terminology; and, despite his careful explanation, his theism, as contrasted with pantheism, sometimes seems to contain a distinction without a difference.

Again and again the American trait of using simple domestic illustrations shifts the level of writing—though this shift is perfectly consistent if we agree that the difference between science and ordinary thinking is but a difference of degree. Homely domestic examples of complex principles merely serve to strengthen this point. The nontechnical reader is refreshed after the corollary of the law of the persistence of force is given "that, in the actions and reactions of force and matter, an unlikeness in either of the factors necessitates an unlikeness in the effects," to have the illustration taken from the kitchen. The point is driven home when we are told that "the crust formed on a loaf of bread or a joint of meat, is due to the necessarily unequal exposure of outside and inside to the incident force coming in shape of heat from the walls of the oven."[23] And there is likewise an oasis for the reader in the delightful little story from Darwin to prove that the cat is a friend and protector of the humblebee. Only the humblebee can fertilize heartsease and red clover: "But observation shows that the mortal foes of humble-bees are field-mice, who destroy their combs and nests. It is estimated that in England more than two-thirds of each generation of humble-bees are destroyed by mice." Finally, "any sensible variation in the number of cats in a given district must indirectly cause a variation in the numbers of heartsease and red clover which grow in the neighborhood."[24] The touch of whimsy underlines the complex rhythms of this lesson in ecology.

Such illustrations are not always so happily chosen, and they jar the reader. We may conjecture that Fiske used them deliberately and consciously, possibly even went out of his way at times to do so. And the evidence for this conclusion is the running banter throughout his letters to his wife on the subject. At times, he reminds her that he likes good, homely phrases; at others, he underlines instances when highly educated people use words which Abby regards as "lowbrow." All in all, Fiske's was a fairly good case of mild revolt against Victorian genteelness, an attempt to keep a little flavor of shaggy roughness for strength of character.

No better way of demonstrating the blend of science and philosophy, objective and subjective, exists than to cite a passage so characteristic that in all of its elements it might be said to be the essence of John Fiske. It comes at the end of a long series of points which prove that thoughts, feelings, sensations, and emotions are interrelated with chemical body changes; and it concludes by implying that God is scientifically proved to exist:

When one takes a country ramble on a pleasant summer's day, one may fitly ponder on the wondrous significance of this law of the transformation of energy. It is wondrous to reflect that all of the energy stored up [in both man-made and natural objects which we pass] . . . is nothing but metamorphosed solar radiance. . . . The grandest conceptions of Dante and Milton are dwarfed in comparison with the truths which science discloses. But it seems to me that we may go further than this, and say we have here reached something deeper than poetry. In the sense of illimitable vastness with which we are oppressed and saddened as we try to follow out in thought the eternal metamorphosis, we may recognize the modern phase of the feeling which led the ancient to fall upon his knees, and adore—after his own crude fashion—the invisible Power whereof the infinite web of phenomena is but the visible garment.[25]

This passage may, indeed, go beyond poetry; but there is much in it that is closer to Emerson and Whitman, even to Jonathan Edwards, than to science per se.

Whatever its ultimate importance in the history of ideas and whatever its influence on the course of American intellectual history, for Fiske himself the completion of the book was a milepost in his Pilgrim's Progress—having revised and modified the lectures, he had now put down his ideas in print as clearly and logically as he was able so that he could determine where he stood. Perhaps for the most part this intention was subconscious, but it summed up for him concisely the ground over which he had traveled and to an extent pointed the direction in which he was to go.

Contemporary reaction to *Cosmic Philosophy* was sharply divided along the lines that could have been predicted with the religious press pointedly and acridly opposed. Fiske himself had quoted Spencer as saying that man was not moved by ideas but by feelings, and emotion was at the base of the critical comment. Clergymen were primarily incensed by the continued denial of special creation, but some of their objections contained a note of satire bordering on sarcasm indicative of a sense of losing ground, a kind of rearguard sniping. The anti-evolutionist fought a bitter fight and still wages guerrilla warfare from mountain strongholds today; but even in the 1870's his voice had a note of despair. Logical arguments gave way to flippancy: "In the continuous redistribution of matter and motion there has at last been evolved, by integration of the homogeneous, the American apostle of the truth hitherto hidden from the eyes of men. A series of states of consciousness (plus a something), resident in Cambridge, has worked over a certain amount of sunshine, and has communicated it to other possibly existing series of states of consciousness in the shape of a book entitled Outlines of Cosmic Philosophy."[26]

Facetious as this statement may appear, there is a certain amount of sting, as there is also in the cartoon from the New York *Graphic* of Professor John Fiske attempting to launch an evolution kite with a tail of animals descending down from the ape. Two apes are reading from the works of Spencer while that worthy would charge across the field with the kite string were it not for a third ape tugging at his coattail.

On the opposite side, the most telling bit of commendation came in a personal letter from Charles Darwin, who had already confessed that he had not understood Spencer until Fiske had translated him. By the time the critical pros and cons appeared, John Fiske had returned to family life in Petersham and Cambridge, to work at the Harvard library, and to become involved soon with lecturing as a historian.

II *Other Philosophical Writings*

Various external events including the exigencies of making a living for an expanding family slowly shifted John Fiske's interest—at least in respect to concrete subject matter—to American history. He discovered a respectably large audience for lectures in that field, and little by little he collected material for later volumes of history. In the meantime, he continued to bring out a number of books closely related to his *Cosmic Philosophy*. At the expense of strict chronology, I should like at this point to examine a series of works directly allied to the philosophy and published over a period of years: *The Unseen World* (1876), *Darwinism and Other Essays* (1879), *The Destiny of Man* (1884), *The Idea of God* (1885), *Through Nature to God* (1889).

Whatever may have been the critical reactions to his first published philosophical work, there are at least two good reasons to suppose that it did, indeed, create much interest. First of all, each of the other collections in this area is heavily focused on restating ideas which first appeared in *Cosmic Philosophy*. Fiske was at great pains, again and again, to explain what he had meant; to point up the places where he had been misunderstood: it was all so very clear and simple, and withal so wonderfully awe-inspiring—if people could only be made to see. The tone of these subsequent books makes it clear that he was getting a good deal of response to his ideas—people might not agree, and they might seriously misinterpret, but at least they were paying attention. Second, on a less elevated level, several of these volumes were collections of essays heavily fortified by reprints of magazine articles. It is doubtful that a publisher would have risked bringing out such heterogeneous assemblages unless there had been a fairly good Fiske market. *The Unseen World and Other Essays,* for example, ranges all the way from the title essay through such things as a pair of essays on Jesus to reviews of John Knowles Paine's Saint Peter Oratorio and of Longfellow's translation of Dante. With amazing naïveté or candor, Fiske concludes the dedication to James Sime: "As for the dozen papers which I have appended to it, by way of clearing out my workshop, I hope you will read them indulgently. . . ."

Toward the end of the title essay there is a passage which does more than all of the critical analysis we could write to show what was truly John Fiske in all of this writing about science and philosophy. The paragraph is a variation on the theme already set forth in the philosophy. Fiske grants that the picture displayed by science of giant worlds concentrating out of nebulous vapor holds little that is intellectually satisfying. "A senseless bubble-play of Titan forces, with life, love and aspiration brought forth only to be extinguished," is cause for human despair. Even the scientifically trained mind must recoil from such a conclusion: "And there are moments when one feels that this cannot be all. On warm June mornings, in green country lanes, with sweet pine-odours wafted in the breeze which sighs in the branches, while little birds sing their love songs over far-off blue mountains . . .

> One far-off divine event
> To which the whole creation moves."[27]

The scientific picture is sharper and more apparently meaning-less than the parallel in *Cosmic Philosophy*; the nature scene is prettier and less scientific. But the inner thought is unchanged: science can portray only what is known, to see or believe in what lies beyond requires an act of faith—but an act of faith based on knowledge and therefore science.

The village atheist? The Harvard student whose ideas were antireligious? Yet this voice is the same with which Fiske had spoken all along, dangerous as Emerson was dangerous; atheist as Wordsworth was atheist. Earlier this note had been muted, and the focus had been on the answers which science could give. But even when his attention was on intellectual questions, Fiske began with the assumption that there are limitations to the human mind, that science can deal only with the known or the knowable. The basic assumption (or spiritual reservation) was passed over quickly—or became lost in the convolutions of two volumes of Cosmism. In this essay of less than sixty pages, it comes more sharply into focus. He begins with the classic Homeric questions: "What are you, where did you come from, and whither are you bound?" From this point, by means of de-tailed astronomical and physical description of the universe that science can reveal, he removes the whole question from the realm of science. This method was later to become the basis of his dis-missal of the conflict between science and religion: there are things we cannot know, and with these science does not attempt to deal. Thus we are brought to a conclusion which sounds remarkably orthodox in the mid-twentieth century: "Believing, however, through a simple act of trust, that the end will crown the work, we may rise superior to the question which has here concerned us, and exclaim, in the supreme language of faith, 'Though He slay me, yet will I trust in Him.' "[28] I am man; I come from God knows where; I am bound wherever He wills.

Had this emotional quality dominated from the first, the response might have been different—but then it would not have been heard above the attack on theology. While Fiske's opponents could not legitimately cry out "atheist," his views, as far as they were concerned, came to the same thing. In spite of the language, what Fiske is saying is a ground for challenge: God is unknowable and cannot be reduced to a being, a sense of his Power is through nature and art, not the Bible—a book of historic events, myths, and ancient tribal laws. Many others had argued as Fiske was doing: Theodore Parker preached similar ideas in Boston in 1841; it was the main theme of Fiske's own distinction between the Jesus of history and the Christ of dogma; and he repeated the argument in a symposium with several clergymen in 1878. For John Fiske, making a fetish of the Bible was irreverent: "The spiritual import of this wonderful collection of writings becomes its most important aspect; and, freed from the exigencies of a crude philosophy and an insane criticism, the Bible becomes once more the book of mankind."[29] He may have found the abstraction of Absolute, infinite, eternal (explicitly defined) awe-ful to behold; but the church preferred, at least symbolically, God the Father, one not too much more remote than the mighty figure of Michelangelo's *Last Judgment*.

Darwinism and Other Essays is a similar collection, but, on the whole, it is more closely integrated than the previous volume. Such collections present some difficulty for the modern biographer who is attempting to trace the development of Fiske's thought since they pay little attention to the chronology of when the individual essays were first written. This particular collection was modified in the second edition of 1885 by the inclusion of three additional essays, one of which was the article on Buckle first published when the author was nineteen. However, were all the essays untangled and laid end to end according to the dates of conception, we would be forcefully reminded that the human mind does not move in a straight line. Like most of us, Fiske might be said to think somewhat in spirals, returning again and again to earlier thoughts but never quite on the same plane.

As we have noted, John Fiske gave the major portion of his time and attention to a study of history. He did not, however, neglect completely either science or philosophy. As the years passed many of the clergy came to admire his viewpoint; at their invitation, he took over their pulpits for his Sunday sermons. An exaggeration, perhaps, but generally it is true that Fiske tended to mark time while opinion slowly came around to his position.

In 1884, Bronson Alcott's Concord School invited Fiske to take part in a series of lectures about man's immortality from various philosophical or theological points of view. Presumably, Fiske was to represent the materialist view, although he accepted the invitation as an opportunity to dissociate himself from this position. The lecture he presented, later published as *The Destiny of Man*, was precisely what a student of Fiske might have expected. He began with a historical pattern sketching the view of the universe held in the Middle Ages and most beautifully exemplified by Dante, the need for adjustment of this view in the face of the discoveries of Copernicus, and the equally sweeping need for adjustment in the face of the new science of Lyell and Darwin. Fiske then turned to a description of the universe as seen by modern science, and the portrait is not notably different from that in his *Cosmic Philosophy*. What difference there is is of degree and of tone rather than of kind. He still points out the immeasurable vastness and variety, but now the emphasis is on order and unity in accordance with immutable law.

And he ends with a thought he had expressed before, though probably never quite so sharply stated: "I believe it has been fully shown that so far from degrading Humanity, or putting it on a level with the animal world in general, the doctrine of evolution shows us distinctly for the first time how the creation and perfecting of Man is the goal toward which Nature's work has been tending from the first. We can now see clearly that our new knowledge enlarges tenfold the significance of human life, and makes it seem more than ever the chief object of Divine care, the consummate fruition of that creative energy which is manifested throughout the knowable universe."[30]

To admit, immediately after this statement, that science could neither affirm nor deny the immortality of man is not to eradicate the most unscientific implications that Fiske had already read in: for science could no more affirm nor deny that evolution was necessarily progress; that the Infinite, Eternal Power exists; nor that man is the crowning glory of His work. But John Fiske was acclaiming these very things—and building an elaborate framework of logic and scientific evidence to support them.

Largely the argument turns on a negative point: "The material-
istic assumption . . . that the life of the soul ends with the life of
the body, is perhaps the most colossal instance of baseless
assumption that is known to the history of philosophy. . . . With
his illegitimate hypothesis of annihilation, the materialist trans-
gresses the bounds of experience quite as widely as the poet
who sings of the new Jerusalem with its rivers of life and its
streets of gold. Scientifically speaking, there is not a particle
of evidence for either view."[31] True enough, but Fiske both by
temperament and in his desire to be rid of the materialist label,
decidedly favored the poet, if only metaphorically.

Yet if we pay full attention to all of the qualifying statements, the argument itself is sound enough. Probably it does
contain a number of interpretations presented as if they were
facts; and, like all arguments, it begins with assumptions.
However, it ends not as a scientific declaration but as a confession of faith; it is "old wine in new bottles." Removing the
whole argument from the realm of science (well, almost), Fiske
concludes: "For my own part, therefore, I believe in the immortality of the soul, not in the sense in which I accept the
demonstrable truths of science, but as a supreme act of faith
in the reasonableness of God's work."[32] This view, he maintains,
has survived both the Copernican and the Darwinian revolu-
tions. In fact, Darwinism is responsible for man's finding himself on a higher pinnacle than ever before: "The future is
lighted for us with the radiant colors of hope. Strife and sorrow shall disappear. Peace and love shall reign supreme. The
dream of poets, the lesson of priest and prophet, the inspiration
of the great musician, is confirmed in the light of modern
knowledge; and as we gird ourselves up for the work of life,
we may look forward to the time when in the truest sense the
kingdoms of this world shall become the kingdom of Christ, and
he shall reign for ever and ever, king of kings and lord of lords."[33]

Nothing could have been more comforting to those of Fiske's
contemporaries who were willing to be comforted—the new
science was not so frightening after all. But, ironically for the
man who had been labeled a young radical, nothing could have
been less helpful to those of the coming generation. John Fiske
might take the panoramic view, but they saw only the world
around them. He might feel that, with science and religion recon-

ciled, there was every reason for the man of science to echo the
language of the Bible; but too many of them heard the same
message they had been taught in Sunday School. It was undoubtedly not only the traditional language but the optimistic cry of
progress—and Fiske maintained it even when conditions made
it necessary for him to reiterate that truth would prevail only
in the long run—which put him out of touch with the rising
generation.

Fiske's message did not move the young men and women
who became the muckrakers, who could not see God's good
design in robber barons, who remembered that Andrew Carnegie
had also been devoted to Spencer, and who observed that the
survival of the fittest had caught at the phase of nature red in
tooth and claw and was not advancing to the fittest in any
intellectual, psychological, or spiritual sense that they could
see. It was on this optimistic cry of inevitable progress that
Fiske demanded noninterference, that he held to a laissez faire
belief in economics and government, at a time when the younger
generation demanded an attempt at a controlled universe.

Even Spencer had his reservations to some of the religious
implications: "you approach more nearly to a positive conclusion
than I feel inclined to do. Have you ever looked into W. R.
Greg's later essays? In one of these he, in a very interesting
way, discusses the question of immortality: implying that in his
own case, the desire for continued life wanes as age advances,
and the desire becomes rather that for absolute rest."[34] The
strongest response to *The Destiny of Man* came not so much
from the reviews as in private letters which clearly indicated
that many people had found in Fiske a comforting solution
which allowed them to retain an intellectual acceptance of science, to reject the orthodox theology with which science was
at war, and to find themselves still spiritually sound—and on a
higher plane than before. In any case, *The Destiny of Man*
drew sufficient interest for the directors of the school to invite
Fiske to lecture a second year, in 1885; and this time the choice
of topic was his own. The topic he chose was *The Idea of God
as Affected by Modern Knowledge*.

The second Concord lecture is admittedly a new piece of
work, not a repetition of the one before it; nevertheless, the
pattern is similar, the assumptions and conclusions ultimately

the same. In his preface, Fiske himself accurately measures the similarity and the difference: although his views had undergone no such radical change as some of the readers of *The Destiny of Man* suggested, "It would be little to my credit, however, had my views of the doctrine of evolution and its implications undergone no development or enlargement.... To carry such a subject about in one's mind for ten years, without having any new thoughts about it, would hardly be proof of fitness for philosophizing." Yet, "nothing of fundamental importance in 'Cosmic Philosophy' needs changing."[35] And the second lecture is a sequel to the first: "the two books taken together, contain the bare outlines of a theory of religion."

With an echo—or prevision—of Henry Adams' idea of acceleration, Fiske considers the nineteenth century to be in the midst of a mighty revolution in human thought. In a series of illustrations he graphically sketches the increasing rate of material progress, noting that our minds have become so deadened by the real import that his examples have an air of triteness. "We scarcely need to be reminded that all the advances made in locomotion, from the days of Nebuchadnezzar to those of Andrew Jackson, were as nothing compared to the change that has been wrought within a few years by the introduction of the railroads." In an age when electricity sends a message around the earth in forty minutes, his listeners need to be reminded that it is scarcely a century since the death of Franklin, "who caught the lightning upon his kite." And grandmother's spinning wheel, still standing by the fireside, should be a reminder that "the change therein exemplified since Penelope plied her distaff is far less than that which has occurred within the memory of living man."[36] Beyond the material, having surveyed the history of the concepts of God through the ages, he finds most drastic changes resulting from the overwhelming increase in the area of human knowledge—knowledge which, since the dawn of consciousness, has been advancing in geometric progression.

Part of this lecture is one of the clearest and simplest statements that has been set forth on what is now considered the Victorian dilemma:

No religious creed that man has ever devised can be made to harmonize in all its features with modern knowledge. All such creeds were constructed with reference to theories of the universe which are now utterly and hopelessly discredited. How, then, it is asked, amid the general wreck of old beliefs, can we hope that the religious attitude in which from time immemorial we have been wont to contemplate the universe can any longer be maintained? Is not the belief in God perhaps a dream of the childhood of our race, like the belief in elves and bogarts which once were no less universal? and is not modern science fast destroying the one as it has already destroyed the other?[37]

As a man who had early seen the implications of science and made use of them in working out a philosophy for himself, Fiske tried to give both a warning and an answer. He insisted that the great fears of his contemporaries were in one way solidly founded: the old beliefs were dead, and there was no return. But fear was not the right emotion, for out of the old arose the new. But the new was perplexing to the simple mind because of the grandeur and vastness, a concept of God freed from all anthropomorphic imagery, a concept which made room for growth of knowledge until the edge of infinity, yet deepened rather than challenged belief: "The everlasting source of phenomena is none other than the infinite Power that makes for righteousness. Thou canst not by searching find Him out; yet put thy trust in Him, and against thee the gates of hell shall not prevail; for there is neither wisdom nor understanding nor counsel against the Eternal."[38]

In reviewing *The Destiny of Man*, Fiske's dear friend Howells had found "Mr. Fiske unable to language his thoughts of infinity at supreme moments except in the words of the old Book of those Semitic tribes so remote from Darwin."[39] In all probability, Howells wrote with a smile; for he knew Fiske well enough to be aware of the difference—a difference which so precisely tells why Fiske's metaphor had to be organic. Fiske's was, indeed, the old language; but only as the fruit is the bud from which it grew. Fiske continued to use the same kind of language in what, for all practical purposes, was his final word on religion, *Through Nature to God*, published in 1889.

The last of these philosophical books is divided into three parts: "The Mystery of Evil," "The Cosmic Roots of Love and Self-Sacrifice," and "The Everlasting Reality of Religion." Here, among many of the old premises, painstakingly rephrased, he

attempts to come face to face with what must have been contemporary challenges to his religious argument. Nowhere else
has he so firmly looked at evil or the slayer and the slain; nowhere else has he so clearly realigned himself with his past—
with Calvinism and with Emerson and Parker. Although Fiske
maintains that evil must remain a mystery, he finds two possible
views which may be adopted, or have been adopted through
history. One of these, most recently and cogently set forth by
John Stuart Mill, cannot imagine God to have created evil and
therefore sets up a dualism which curtails God's omnipotence:
"God's creative power has been limited by some inexplicable
viciousness in the original constitution of things."

But Fiske himself prefers the thinking of the seventeenth-
century Calvinist, who "might well say that the God which
Mr. Mill offers us, shorn of the attribute of omnipotence, is no
God at all. He would say with the Hebrew prophet, that God
has created the evil along with the good, and that he has done
so for a purpose which human reason, could it at once comprehend all the conditions of the case, would most surely approve
as infinitely wise and holy." Nor is it particularly startling to
those who have read Fiske's earlier work when he adds that
"the Calvinist would declare that if we really understood the
universe we should find scientific justification of the victorious
cry of faith, 'Though He slay me, yet will I trust in Him!' The
man who has acquired such faith as this is the true freeman
of the universe, . . . whose guerdon is the serene happiness that
can never be taken away."[40] This view is a far cry from the
man who wrote to his fiancée in 1862, "I detest Calvinistic orthodoxy with my whole soul. I had rather be a *Buddhist* than a
presbyterian. Calvin himself was about the most abominable
old scamp that ever disgraced this mundane orb with his presence. I look upon him as a sort of incarnation of the Devil he
talks about."[41] The scars of wounds inflicted by the Reverend
Jeremiah Taylor had at last healed.

The solution Fiske offers to the question of evil is, of course,
the age-old argument of contrasts: without evil how can we
measure good? Complete innocence is equivalent to ignorance
and can have no basis for moral judgment. For several pages
he attempts to suggest the scientific truth behind this. The
premise is that scientific experience bears out the concept of

the unity of nature. If nature is unified, then the analogy between the physical world and the psychical world is justified
since both are aspects of nature. Therefore a proof drawn from
the physical world will be paralleled in the psychical world. In
a world of unqualified redness we would be unaware of color,
just as we are unaware of the pressure of atmosphere upon our
bodies unless we climb a mountain and experience a contrast
in pressure. So, too, "in a happy world there must be sorrow
and pain, and in a moral world the knowledge of evil is indis-
pensable"; for otherwise there is no means by which consciousness can make distinctions.

That the world is moral and ultimately happy is taken for
granted. However solid this reasoning may or may not be
logically or scientifically, the tradition of New England Puritanism rises from deep in Fiske's nature as he concludes the chapter: "What would have been the moral value of a race of human
beings ignorant of sin and doing beneficent acts with no more
consciousness or volition than the deftly contrived machine
that picks up raw material at one end, and turns out some
finished product at the other? Clearly, for strong and resolute
men and women an Eden would be but a fool's paradise. How
could anything fit to be called *character* have ever been produced there? But for tasting the forbidden fruit, in what respect
could man have become a being of higher order than the beasts
of the field?"[42]

At this point, Fiske pauses for a note of shocked amusement
that, when he had offered this theory earlier, some had understood it "as a glorification of sin, and an invitation to my fellow-
men to come forth with me and be wicked!" There were even
those who asked "just what percentage of sin and crime I regarded as needful for the moral equilibrium of the universe;
how much did I propose to commit myself, and just where
would I have them stop!"[43] John solemnly adds that God has
provided sufficient evil and the duty of man is to suppress it;
for, in full faith in the perfectibility of man, he sees the day
far distant when God's purpose is achieved and the needed
contrast between good and evil will be supplied by memory
rather than by fact.

The most intriguing portion of the book is a little chapter
called "The Summer Field, and what it tells us," for it con-

trasts the zenith and the nadir of man's view of nature. Fiske has never gone further toward presenting graphically and concretely a universe controlled by blind chance, though, of course, he entirely rejects the idea. We are given two word pictures of a field of daisies in June, and the first, while entirely Fiske's own painting, is a charming parallel for Lowell's "What is so rare as a day in June...." The entire picture carries a tone of Victorian sentiment which would be cloying to the modern were it not for the unconscious artistry which balances it against the second picture. As we look a little closer, we find this summer field to be a battleground of butchery and destruction, "of robbery utterly shameless and murder utterly cruel."[44] He ends with "the hawk's talons buried in the breast of the wren, while the relentless beak tears the little wings from the quivering, bleeding body...." And this carnage, he concedes, is the process of evolution: "but for the pitiless destruction of individuals that fall short of a certain degree of fitness... the type would inevitably degenerate, the life would become lower and meaner in kind." For, he adds, "The principle of natural selection is in one respect intensely Calvinistic; it elects the one and damns the ninety and nine."[45]

But Fiske also concedes that "Evolution and progress are not synonymous terms. The survival of the fittest is not always the survival of the best or of the most highly organized." Turning his attention to human beings, he reserves "transcendently important qualifications" to be considered later; but, for the moment, he notes that the development of civilization on its political side has been a stupendous struggle in which the possession of certain attributes has allowed some tribes or nations to subject or exterminate others. And he touches upon the whole question of the Robber Barons:

On its industrial side the struggle has been no less fierce; the evolution of higher efficiency through merciless competition is a matter of common knowledge. Alike in the occupations of war and in those of peace, superior capacity has thriven upon victories in which small heed has been paid to the wishes or the welfare of the vanquished. In human history perhaps no relation has been more persistently repeated than that of the hawk and the wren. The aggression has usually been defended as in the interests of higher civilization, and in the majority of cases the defense has been sustained by the facts.

It has indeed very commonly been true that the survival of the strongest is the survival of the fittest. . . . Upon such a view as this the Cosmic Process appears in a high degree unintelligent, not to say immoral.[46]

However, Fiske has already stated in his preface that he intends to try to reply to Huxley's Romanes Lecture. As Fiske summarizes it, Huxley's argument seemed to say that there was a duality—the amoral cosmic process and the ethical process—and that social progress depended not on imitating the cosmic process, still less running away from it, but in combating it. But if, says Fiske, Huxley were still alive, he would agree that he was using the phrase "cosmic process" in two senses: one, as a synonym for "natural selection," otherwise known as "survival of the fittest"; two, the over-all process of which natural selection is but a part. In respect to the narrower concept of survival of the fittest, as Fiske has already admitted, there is indeed no morality involved; but the "cosmic process is ethical in the profoundest sense, that in that far-off morning of the world, when the stars sang together and the sons of God shouted for joy, the beauty of self-sacrifice and disinterested love formed the chief burden of the mighty theme."[47]

The proof of the basic morality and concern for self-sacrifice is the repeated argument of prolonged human infancy. Based solidly on the preservation of the species (protection of the helpless young), the nobler feelings of humanity come into being. This development is the cosmic process, and thus we have come full circle: the moral goal is the building of human character and all things contribute toward this goal. By means of a quotation from Emerson, Fiske reminds us, however, that art—whether man's or God's—is long: "the lesson of life . . . is to believe what the years and centuries say against the hours; to resist the usurpation of particulars; to penetrate to their catholic sense."[48]

The book ends rather quietly on a note which underscores all that Fiske had been trying to do: "But we have at length reached a stage where it is becoming daily more and more apparent that with the deeper study of nature the old strife between faith and knowledge is drawing to a close; and disentangled at last from that ancient slough of despond the Human Mind will breathe a freer air and enjoy a vaster horizon."[49] This final sentence indicates that John Fiske believed the time had come for writing "Quod erat demonstrandum." The problem had been to prove that science was not and never had been in conflict with religion—that science was actually a confirmation of man's higher visions. Had Fiske indeed achieved such a goal, his position would be eternally secure. He hoped he had, and some of his friends believed he had; but the doubts and fears of Matthew Arnold's *Dover Beach* continue to echo down the years.

As we look back over the long history of Fiske's philosophical writings, we are inclined to apply his own organic metaphor to the development of his ideas; for they most certainly did not spring forth full blown. But whether we take the seed-to-flower analogy or not, one note needs to be struck. About two-thirds of the way through the first volume of *Cosmic Philosophy,* Fiske described the over-all process as made up of two counter-processes of Evolution and Dissolution; at that point he set aside with good reason the dissolution, but there was no scientific or logical reason for doing so forever. Literally, he speaks of it again in projecting the "probable future disintegration of our planetary system," but he tosses the argument to infinity and eternity and thus beyond the range of science: "At the outermost verge to which scientific methods can guide us, we can only catch a vague glimpse of a stupendous rhythmical alternation between eras of Evolution and eras of Dissolution, succeeding each other 'without vestiges of a beginning and without prospect of an end.' "[50]

This conclusion, of course, is a perfectly legitimate one for the scientist; nevertheless, if he is also going to be a prophet, he must needs deal with both phases of the larger process. It is, of course, true that the seed does ripen into flower—but so too does the flower ripen into fruit, and the fruit to decay, and so on. In shifting emphasis, as Fiske does in these religious writings, to focus upon man as the ultimately unfolded flower, so to speak, he leaves unconsidered the rest, the dissolution. To use his own terms: it is inconceivable that the process can be at one and the same time cyclical and aimed, as a line, at a goal. Nor does it help very greatly to imply that the cycle is so vast that the given arc which we can comprehend might as well be a straight line.

This statement is intended not as a criticism of Fiske but

as a mere suggestion as to the basic cause of the failure of his philosophy. In the long run, Fiske's message left the dichotomies as strong as he had found them. And, in his deeper wisdom, he must have known that he did so since he knew so well the vast chasm that existed between the known and the unknown, the experience of man and the infinite, eternal absolute of God. He had tried his best to achieve a cosmic view; but, in the end, Fiske echoes Spencer's insistence that a kind of synthesis was the best that could be expected.

CHAPTER 4

The Lecture Circuit

I *Early Lecturing Career*

ALTHOUGH John Fiske's appointment as assistant librarian at Harvard had been made permanent in 1873, it is difficult to believe that his heart was really in the work; in his own mind, it was doubtless but a means of staying there until something developed in the history department. While in Europe, he had visited a number of libraries; but he appears to have given them a rather cursory study and always with the conclusion that the Harvard system was better. And his one essay on the workings of a library is a rather pedestrian affair designed largely to add its small contribution to his income. Weighing the evidence carefully, we conclude that he did a thoroughly competent job; but, except for some of his solutions to cataloguing, he made no brilliant contribution.

On the one hand, when Fiske applied in January, 1875, for an increase in salary, the board agreed to $2,500 annually plus an annual bonus of $500 "in recognition of exceptionally arduous and important service": the bonus was a device for keeping his nominal salary lower than that of the chief librarian. Also there is testimony from reliable authorities, such as Charles K. Bolton of the Boston Athenaeum, that Fiske was a remarkably fine cataloguer. However, in the summer of 1877, when the chief librarian resigned, there was no question of promoting Fiske; rather, a good deal of searching was done, and the appointment went to Justin Winsor, historian and professional librarian. The fact may well be that President Eliot agreed that Fiske's true place was in the history department rather than that Fiske had limitations as a librarian.

During the period between Fiske's return from Europe and his withdrawal from the library, there was considerable dickering in respect to a professorial appointment. While giving a course of lectures in Baltimore in the late winter of 1877, John wrote to Abby a careful report about Johns Hopkins which gives every indication that he had been, or expected to be, offered a position there. But only a month later he informs his mother that he cannot bear the thought of leaving Cambridge. Perhaps he had already been informed of Henry Adams' imminent resignation which came in April.

By July, when the chief librarian tendered his resignation, Fiske could further inform his mother that two young instructors were filling in for Adams for one year; and, at the end of that time, it was intended to move Fiske into the history department. Hindsight and a knowledge of academic politics make it perfectly clear that this appointment was not to be; possibly an objective observer could have seen this fact even at the time, but Fiske continued to hope a while longer. These developments made him impatient with the library: "I hope another year will free me from this blasted old library which has throttled and suffocated my original work for now nearly seven years of my life. I seriously contemplate resigning" (November, 1878).[1]

The following January Fiske refused a bid to become a professor at the College of the City of New York, and a good deal of light is thrown on the situation by his letter to Harvard board member Edward E. Hale in April. Clearly, Fiske felt that there were two problems involved: first, the old opposition to his religious views hung in the air; and he explains again that he is not and never was a positivist or an atheist, adding rather petulantly, "To anyone who really knew my state of mind as to religious matters, there never could have been a more ridiculous comedy—even supposing that the question was any of their business, which of course it wasn't." Second, his recent activities outside the college had suggested that his interest lay in American colonial history, now taught by Henry Cabot Lodge; but, Fiske assured Hale, his deepest interest lay in medieval history "and that is why I have such an extreme longing for the place which Adams left vacant."[2] Apparently this letter was a last desperate attempt to explain, for in February John Fiske resigned from the library and turned his attention to lecturing.

The months between Henry Adams' departure from Harvard

and John Fiske's resignation from the library no doubt carried their frustrations, but it was not a dull period in the Fiske household. In August, 1877, Herbert Huxley Fiske, the fourth son and last child, was born. The entire autumn was full of the activities of building a new house at 22 Berkeley Street, almost in Longfellow's back yard; and Fiske surveyed the whole process from digging the foundation to building the library shelves. At the end of the year, he was present at the now famous Whittier dinner and commented briefly, "Apart from Mark Twain's speech which was a ghastly mistake, the occasion was great. There was a tremendous spread and Howells was in fine feather."[3]

The following summer included a delightful visit to Celia Thaxter at Appledore, an opportunity for boating and music, both of which Fiske loved. And among these social activities, Fiske found time for exploring Harvard library's material about American colonial history—evidently, the task of cataloguing some of this material drew his attention to the field; and his discovery that the library records allowed him to trace the Fiske genealogy back some twelve generations made him aware of the potential of such work. During his last few months, he did one of his best cataloguing jobs on Harvard's excellent collection of modern Greek books with some assistance from charming old Professor Sophocles. And, to wind up our heterogeneous survey of Fiske's activities, he began the study of Russian. Fiske delighted in variety.

If, as Fiske had suggested to Hale, there was truly any confusion about the area of history in which Fiske was interested, it arose directly from an extracurricular project in which he was engaged. As early as 1872 his cataloguing work in the library's American room had first awakened his interest in American history. Early in 1878 he was invited to give a series of lectures in Boston to aid in raising funds for saving the Old South Church. Working during the summer on the preparation of these lectures brought his old love of history to the surface, and he found the possibilities of interpreting American history against his evolutionary philosophy so exciting that it opened up a whole new career. Encouraged by such friends as Francis Parkman, John confidently took the plunge; and in February, 1879, as we have noted, he resigned his position as librarian. There is something to be said of the courage—or foolhardiness—of a man who would dare such an act. It left him without regular income and with a wife and six children to support. And, indeed, he at one point came close to financial disaster even with Mr. Stoughton and James Brooks in the background. Fiske's instincts, however, proved in the long run to have been right—we only regret that he had not earlier turned his back on the temptations of academic preferment at Harvard.

The lectures on "America's Place in History" were "a brilliant success." The phrase is a standard one, for it is repeated again and again in comments on Fiske lectures through the years; sometimes it represents mere journalistic politeness or formal praise; sometimes it is whistling in the dark; sometimes it is true. In his initial venture with history, fate gave John Fiske a full house. He himself was in fine form, his subject was right, his audience was the kind he most appealed to, and his theme was one they needed to hear. Regularly, Americans were being told by European visitors of their shortcomings; all the way from Sidney Smith's "who reads an American book?" to visitors Mrs. Trollope, Dickens, and Arnold, our English cousins found us wanting. For a long time American faith and excitement about the future made it possible to care little about the past, but at least on some levels of society these attacks were beginning to irritate. Now, John Fiske, who had a reputation as a scholar and a student of history, could say quietly but firmly that "The voyage of Columbus was in many respects the most important event in human history since the birth of Christ." This fact, of course, Americans had always known; but perhaps Fiske could explain it to the rest of the world.

And, as a matter of fact, to tell the world is precisely what John Fiske did. He told the same thing to the British (who else mattered?) and made them love it. Urged by Mrs. Hemenway, who had initially been responsible for the series, John contacted friends in England offering to repeat the lectures there; the reply was "Come." Once again Fiske tumbled aboard a steamer and set out for his second home. Once again he must have been financed by a guardian angel, for, in a letter reporting his success, Abby is reminded to relay the news to "my fairy godmother, Mrs. Hemenway."[4]

Once again we have delightful letters home full of places and people, this time including sketches not only of his English friends but of Henry James, Henry Adams, and Turgenev, who was "not unlike Longfellow in appearance." From the outset, Fiske had not planned on any financial return from the series of lectures; the all-important thing was to achieve a great success in audience response and probably newspaper notice; for there was nothing like fame in England to attract American audiences to future lectures. But not until the very last minute could he be sure of any success at all.

On the day of the first presentation, there came an "American rain," a regular downpour. He may be using hyperbole, but he writes that at 2:50 the hall was all but empty while by 3:05 there was an audience of some four hundred; and evidently they were "*the* four hundred." The series was auspiciously launched, and for the concluding lecture Fiske had people standing in the aisles. What did one say to an English audience that could arouse such enthusiasm for their erstwhile colonies? Unquestionably, it was the final oration that really gained attention, a little gem called "The Manifest Destiny of the English Race." The main thesis of Fiske's interpretation of American history was that it was a continuation of the history of England. He used the concept of evolution to prove that, from old Germanic forms of government through English patterns to the New England town meeting and American federalism, the best political form was slowly developing. With her English heritage, America had solved the political problem. Ultimately, the influence of Anglo-American political ideas would civilize the world.

His letter home reveals the key to English enthusiasm. He might almost be accused of shrewd showmanship except that we cannot doubt that the lectures had not been changed since delivery at home—and they had not been designed originally for a British response. Fiske firmly and sincerely believed in his thesis as he demonstrated by the illustration of the dreadful war the British were at that moment waging in Zululand and his confidence in its outcome. His quiet tone proved to be exactly the right note "for the days when *England is in mourning* for husbands, brothers, sons, slain in horrid warfare with the Zulus, and all England is tender about Africa. . . ." The description captures the essence of Fiske's lecturing approach. He rarely

planned consciously for effect, but set forth his message honestly
and backed by conviction. He was, however, keenly receptive
to audience reaction and instinctively built upon it. And with
this English series, fortuitous as it must have been, his timing
was perfect. The letter goes on:

When I began speaking of the future of the English race in Africa,
I became aware of an immense *silence,* a kind of *breathlessness,* all
over the room—although it had been extremely quiet before. After
three or four more sentences, I heard some deep breathings and
murmurs, and "hushes." All at once, when I came round to the
parallel of the English career in America and Africa, there came up
one stupendous SHOUT,—not a common demonstration of approval,
but a deafening SHOUT of exultation. Don't you wish you could have
been there, darling?—it would have been the proudest moment of
your life.[5]

If the tide had ever been against John Fiske, it had now
turned. There would still be rough sailing ahead—in fact, his
greatest financial crisis lay in the future; but he had found his
own field. We do not have, of course, either moving pictures
or tape recordings to help us in our judgment; but it is clear
that (at least with certain types of audiences) Fiske was meant
to be a lecturer. And so thoroughly was he a man of his times,
or sometimes just a bare step ahead of them, that what he
had to say was challenging and exciting, and he returned to
America to find himself much in demand. To sweeten the
triumph, his friends were at last in the majority at Harvard;
he had been elected a member of the Board of Overseers.

Working out a program for the coming lecture season, John
Fiske chose to open with a group of engagements in Maine.
Whatever else this great state had to offer, it did not in 1879
have large resources of the kind he needed. His opening in
Lewiston was a dismal failure until Bates College, challenged
to prove itself cosmopolitan, rose to help. Portland was little
better, and of Brunswick it can only be said that Bowdoin gave
its all; and, while that may have been extremely high in quality,
it was not great in numbers. The phrase which later became
routine when the reaction was disappointing in numbers (and
therefore in money) is not entirely rationalizing: Fiske reported
his audiences as small but select. As far as we can determine,
this was literally true. The general lecture audience sought

popular culture, defined as entertainment delicately coated with learning. John Fiske offered ideas—a solid classroom lecture which demanded mental alertness and some background. Reading the books based on his lectures, we may not find them profound, we may note a good deal of emotional appeal, but we can see clearly that they were designed to guide and instruct.

Fiske knew well how to lecture in Boston. Comparing two visiting lecturers, he once wrote: "The late Mr. Freeman . . . thought it necessary to instruct his audiences in the rudiments of English history, and he was voted a bore for his pains, when there was so much he might have said to which people would have listened with breathless interest. Tyndall received early warning to talk exactly as he would at the Royal Institution. . . . It was a rare treat to hear him lecture."[6]

However suitable the Royal Institution approach was for Boston, Fiske erred in trying to use it in Maine, whose audiences had been regaled with "How to Shoot Your Grandfather's Ghost." Poor Lewiston little deserved its fate: Fiske could not help making comparisons with Boston and London, and the Maine city became a touchstone. In retrospect, he wrote, "X is a dreary spot but not as bad as Lewiston." At the time he wrote, "Great Scott, Lewiston is the most godforsaken hole I ever did see, everything flat dead; a manufacturing town full of red factories and nothing fit to eat or drink. The town is an abomination of desolation! It rasps and scrapes at every aesthetic fibre in a man till the fibre screams. Never before did I know anything so irredeemably and out-and-out beastly; it's a blot on the face of God's world."[7]

In justice to Lewiston and with amusement at Fiske, we must note the modification of this view when Bates did rally to him: "Well, I dislike the place still for a place to stay in when you are homesick for the dearest wife and sweetest children in the world. Moreover the food at the DeWitt House is enough to make the stoutest *heart* quiver with apprehension, aye, and the stoutest *stomach* too. Lewiston is a sort of inferior edition of Middletown without half the natural beauties."[8] Fiske might have forgiven all the inadequacies, however, had the meals been tempting. Whatever else this first campaign may have proved, it ought to have demonstrated sharply that Professor John Fiske was not a man of the people. Well he might insist that he was for the people and that he believed in the people, but his appeal—like that of Whitman—was to the educated.

But Lewiston could take heart at its honest lack of interest—the philistines were elsewhere. Brooklyn, New York, was a success due to the loyalty of Harvard men for their class. Four of Fiske's Harvard classmates met his appeal with a tremendous response for the course offered in their town. Philadelphians, however, showed so little interest that a small group of believers solicited money and sent it to him because of the importance of his work. But Washington seemed determined to prove that Matthew Arnold was right about America's lack of civilization. Fiske turned his attention to the capital in reply to a letter signed by President Hayes, members of the cabinet, both Massachusetts senators, and other dignitaries. Of the results, we can only report that "there was a very distinguished audience, though not large of fine quality." And he lost money which he could ill afford to spare. In the long run, however, the Washington experience may have paid off more than appears on the surface; Fiske made many friends, including Secretary Carl Schurz; and, whether through a kind of natively shrewd political sense or through buoyant good charm, Fiske discovered friends to be one of the most effective methods of building up lecture tours and audiences. It did no harm to let it be known that he had lectured before the president of the United States and assorted statesmen.

Fiske's itinerary on lecture tours is exhausting just to read about, and between lectures, as he rode on the cars or waited in hotel rooms, he worked on a new series about American political ideas. Some of the trip must have been discouraging and some of it rewarding; all of it should have been both mentally and physically exhausting. But, through it all, John had another English engagement to look forward to—with the Royal Institution of London and with the Edinburgh Philosophical Institute; and this time Abby was to accompany him. Perhaps, after all, there was nothing so wearing about brief jaunts in the northeastern United States to a man who seems almost to have been commuting to England.

Running through Clark's biography of Fiske is a thread of romance—this trip abroad, we can note incidentally, was a great success; but its real importance was as a glorious wedding trip

—a second honeymoon for Abby and John Fiske. It was a reward for a patient and devoted wife to see and share her husband's triumphs—the joy for the husband to play the social lion before his wife, to offer evidence that her sacrifices had not been in vain. Letters to the folks at home are filled with the joys of sharing with Abby the social and scenic delights of England. Chief among these pleasures was a visit with the Huxleys in return for the hospitality they had received from the Fiskes on their journey to America; and perhaps an even greater pleasure was the excursion to the village of Laxfield from which Fiske's ancestors had emigrated, where they were able to visit the house in which Fiskes had lived before departing for Wenham, Massachusetts, in the seventeenth century.

Life as a public lecturer makes varied demands. There is not only the season itself with the problems of arranging a program that will be financially practical but the need to prepare constantly new materials. Additionally, a man like Fiske must occasionally publish new essays, both to keep his name before the public and to advance, if possible, the literary career that was his true goal. Alternately with traveling—and his itinerary now ranged as far south as Baltimore, as far west as Milwaukee —he found himself preparing new lectures and more magazine articles. Before beginning his lecture campaign of 1880-81, he published two essays: "Sociology and Hero Worship" in the *Atlantic* and "The Causes of Persecution" in the *North American Review.*

The former is particularly interesting because of the conflict with his friend William James which throws a good deal of light on the difference between Fiske and the newer pragmatic philosophy of James and (later) Dewey. In October James had written in the *Atlantic* an essay called, "Great Men, Great Thoughts, and the Environment." Up to a point, James had revealed himself to be a good evolutionist but one with reservations. Along the way he raised questions of what made communities change from generation to generation, "that makes the England of Queen Anne so different from the England of Elizabeth." And his answer went back to Carlyle more than to Spencer.[9]

Fiske was primarily upset by the article's attack on Spencer and his disciples to whom, he felt, James owed a debt and therefore more respect. Fiske denied that they had ignored the individual but maintained that sociology is primarily concerned with general truths revealed by "a comparative study of the actions of great masses of men when considered on a scale where matters of individual idiosyncrasy are averaged, and for the purposes of enquiry, are eliminated." Despite its merits, the Great Men theory does not explain history; its real danger from Fiske's point of view is that it opens the way once again to the theory of "special causes"—the bugaboo over which he had fought so long with the theologians.

Furthermore, a Great Men theory tended to deny the Cosmic plan which saw progress as inevitable: the focus could not very well be on a prearranged plan and at the same time depend upon individual action, except as divinely directed. The Great Man must be seen as servant of humanity and the greatest of them stood as "the Memnon Colossi of the human race. No matter in what century or among what people their feet may be placed, around their brows the music of morning and of evening is forever playing."[10] The difference was basically one of emphasis—and not easily detected when Fiske turned his attention to the concrete writing of history. James promptly apologized gracefully if somewhat playfully: "I have received my spanking, and I shouldn't mind having more from the same rod. I kiss the rod that chastises me! It is pleasant to find one who so perfectly endorses all I have to say about the facts and laws of sociology; and reading your last pages has made me more than ever regret that you are not teaching history in college."[11]

There is a pleasant irony which would have amused James, if he had noted it, in the fact that Fiske was at this moment preparing "Heroes of Industry," an introduction to the eighth volume of a series called *The Hundred Greatest Men*. And of two lectures which Mrs. Hemenway requested for the Old South Church in April, one was to be about Samuel Adams. John Fiske had ample opportunity to demonstrate to James that the evolutionists did not neglect the individual and to expound on his own special emphasis on the way in which the interaction between the individual and society really worked.

The story of the lecture season itself is primarily a record of interesting personal experiences. Most prominent is his visit to Haverford College where he was delighted with the response, and we are struck with his descriptions of the rural aspect of a spot which has since been absorbed by greater Philadelphia. Another is his stay at Cornell where he resided in a coed dormitory—a privilege reserved for ministers—and where he has a comment of approval for coeducation, even though (or perhaps because) a number of couples do get married shortly upon graduation. But we are reminded again that the task of lecturing is regarded with mixed feelings: it is clear that, at least in part, Fiske enjoys it immensely especially for its social aspects and for the opportunity to sing and play after the lectures; on the other hand, it does keep him much away from home, and always uppermost is the dream of literary achievement. The desire develops at this time as a plan for a concise history of the American people. In the spring of 1881, he was approached by Harpers with a request for precisely this sort of book; and he was delighted to be engaged in a definite literary task.

That winter there came a great change in the family life. Mr. Stoughton's career had been climaxed with his appointment as ambassador to Russia. Although this appointment was a great political triumph, the climate seriously impaired the judge's health, so that he was forced to resign. In January, 1882, he died; and, by autumn, John's mother had determined to return to Cambridge to make her home. She planned to build a house which, upon her death, might become the Fiske homestead. As satisfactory a long-range plan as this may have been, the various business activities involved ate noticeably into Fiske's study time. But such domestic upheavals usually left John with a desire to slip away and leave his women to work out the details.

First investigating the resources in American history in the British Museum, he proposed to expatriate himself to England; to shut himself up with his work; and, once and for all, to complete his history. The devoted ladies acquiesced, and in January, 1883, John sailed for his fourth and last visit to the mother country. Research materials proved to be more than adequate. Henry Stevens had assured him that the library had a regular tree of knowledge of American history, even including a full account of Matthew Lyon "and every other important subject illustrative of the rise and progress of the American People, not omitting the remarkable case of Timothy Dexter, the author of 'A Pickle for the Knowing Ones.' "[12]

From Fiske's letters home and from the footnotes to published materials, it is easy to deduce that he did, indeed, manage to do a great deal of research on this English visit. Also his social reception was one of usual kindness and cordiality. Nevertheless, John Fiske seemed to have lost his bounce; physically, he was unwell; and for most of the stay he was miserable. Evidently, the physical problems themselves were of a relatively minor nature. However, they aggravated his customary homesickness; he felt the real cure needed was the presence of Abby, and his physician agreed. Since Abby did not feel free to make the trip, John sailed for home in April. Earlier, it had seemed that escape from domestic life was the only way to get work done; now home was the only spot where he could be content —so he departed for the same reason that he had come. Optimistically, he noted that he had collected a wealth of material, that the trip had been indeed invaluable, but there was no place like home for real work. An underlying truth was that Fiske was struggling with a task for which he was temperamentally unsuited.

Work on the history moved slowly. Naturally given to cosmic and panoramic views, Fiske found little by little a growing dissatisfaction with the whole idea of a short history; everything in him demanded a wider sweep. In the meantime, he was amassing more and more material from his lectures; and his growing reputation made him a better and better risk for publishers. The two projects of the lectures and the history began to intertwine and then to emerge as a series of books beginning with the publication of *American Political Ideas* in 1885. Imperceptibly, the center of importance shifted, as John Fiske had determined it would, to his writings. But the lecture bug had bitten—like his adored Dickens, Fiske must have been at least a little bit of an actor—and he was never to be free of appearing on the platform.

II   *The Second Stage*

Any attempt to divide John Fiske's lecture career into periods is more or less arbitrary; it flowed on uninterruptedly from its beginning to the grand project canceled by his death of appearing on the program of the King Alfred Centennial in 1901. However, events in 1885 brought about a temporary change of approach which underscores the kind of lecturer Fiske was and emphasizes the shift to written from spoken materials. Henry Ward Beecher, attending one of the lectures, "The Critical Period in American History," was captivated but promptly pointed out that Fiske's methods were not doing justice to his abilities or to his financial potential. Fiske was keeping his light about half under a bushel, and Beecher proposed calling in a professional adviser: "Such lectures as you are giving should be heard throughout the country, and you need a good manager to make engagements for you. Let me send you my manager, Major J. B. Pond, and you will find what he doesn't know about managing isn't worth knowing."[13]

Major Pond was indeed perceptive; he saw what Beecher (and Fiske himself) had missed. There is no real irony involved but a misunderstanding of definition: Fiske has been labeled by modern historians as chiefly a popularizer, but the very problem that Pond pointed to was the unsuitability of Fiske's lectures for a popular audience. Nowhere is the fact more strongly emphasized that the modern judgment underlines the word "popularizer"' as being used in its best sense; the point is that Fiske served as an interpreter and teacher rather than as original thinker; the term is not meant to suggest one who cheapens ideas or contributes to what has become known as "popular" culture. While the lectures themselves met with success, the scheme devised by Major Pond was, in general, a failure in large part because of the distinction made above.

To meet Major Pond's objection that his lectures were too "high-brow," John proposed a course of four to six lectures on the great campaigns of the Civil War. As window dressing, the lectures were to be illustrated with the aid of a stereopticon, with maps, diagrams, views of towns and fortresses, and portraits. Major Pond was enthusiastic, but hindsight causes us to nod with tongue in cheek. John Fiske had never been an Edward Everett type of orator. Although he surely did appeal to emotion and drama, he did so through the narrative itself and because his essentially written style was supported by his musical voice, not by the conventional posture and gesture school. A clipping from the Boston *Advertiser* reflects Fiske's own view of his method and is probably quite accurate: "Mr. Fiske makes no gestures, and indulges in no highflown rhetoric; but his manner is extremely easy and graceful, and his dramatic method of presentation brings us face to face with persons and events as if we had seen and known them. . . . Part of the effect, no doubt, is due to the surpassing beauty of his language."[14] And now to involve himself in a perfectly legitimate but still theatrical set of appurtenances of diagrams and a stereopticon? For the scholarly man who had always been able to assume a reasonable knowledge and background in his audience? For the writer who firmly believed that clarity and lucidity of argument were the hallmarks of his lectures? No, it would not work.

Not that the new series did not provide the needed appeal to promise success on the popular circuit. When Fiske opened the series in Boston in November to enthusiastic audiences, applications came in from as far west as Denver, so that it was no problem for Major Pond to arrange a tour lasting until the following May. The first six weeks were confined to New England, but still the taxing schedule often included two lectures a day and whatever hotel accommodations could be wangled. We do not wish to argue that John Fiske could not have gained a popular audience in the wider sense, but it became very clear to him that this strenuous activity was not the way to pay for the freedom of developing his literary career. He did the job well enough, but the price was too high.

John Spencer Clark accurately hits the problem with his comment that the program "deprived him of social intercourse with kindred minds." This program under Major Pond was like life on the vaudeville circuit to one who was accustomed to travel like an opera star on grand tour. Most important, it left no time for writing; but, if such a sacrifice had to be made, Fiske needed at least the relaxation of pleasant musical evenings and comfortable hotel arrangements; for such things were essential to his personal well-being. The strain told physically; a severe cold worsened into pneumonia and forced him home for several weeks in bed. During his convalescence, John had the prudence to see the error and to withdraw from Major Pond's scheme. He would return to the old practice of lecturing at his convenience, subservient to his historical writing. That this diagnosis is reasonably accurate is attested to by the fact that Fiske kept the Civil War lectures on his program and that, in a later presentation (again under his own method of lecturing), they brought commendation from both Union and Confederate officers, particularly from Gen. William Sherman, who commented upon "the tactical as well as the strategic knowledge embodied in them."[15] Depending in part on his prodigious memory, John was making capital of the days in college when his part in the Civil War was to follow campaigns meticulously on the maps hung on the walls of his room.

By 1887, Fiske had consolidated his ideas about the Revolution and the Critical Period, and he was deep in analysis of Europe in the sixteenth and seventeenth centuries for background for *The Beginnings of New England*. For Fiske, history was a matter of cause and effect; and he began well back in time in order to demonstrate the causes of events in the period under consideration. He lifted his lecturing sights now to range as far as California and Oregon. As with the first trip to Europe, the initial impact of new scenery had its effect—he would have said upon his soul. More conservatively, I will suggest, upon his esthetics and his emotions and, through these, upon his history itself. It is hard to call a man with so apparent a cosmopolitan turn a provincial, but in the mid-nineteenth century a familiarity with London was for a bostonian (or Cantabrigian by adoption) little better than a more intimate knowledge of home. Since Fiske's eyes had been mostly focused on the East, the scenery and the people of the Far West widened his horizons. Its vastness and its grandeur could not help but strike sharply on the vision of a man who thought in cosmologies. Sweeping westward on the railroads, he wrote pages of description which still magically capture the imagination of the easterner about the geographical and esthetic majesty of the United States.

The Rockies, of course, were magnificent; but then he had seen both the mountains of Scotland and the Alps for comparison. Oregon and the Columbia left him without comparison, and he even forgot to contrast them with Petersham. But perhaps for a New Englander the endless prairie between Council Bluffs and Cheyenne made the most profound impression: "Utter loneliness, save for now and then a few horses or cows grazing. Sometimes a little undulation, but generally flat as a floor. Railroad track straight as a ruler mile after mile without a curve. After a couple of hundred miles this begins to work upon one's mind powerfully: I began to have an awe-struck feeling, as if I were coming into contact with Infinity. I had taken Tolstoi's 'War and Peace' to read, and it is one of the most powerful stories I ever read, and about on as gigantic a scale as 'Les Misérables.' Somehow the story fitted the landscape, and both worked upon me at once."[16] No other experience could so vividly have confirmed his sense of the importance of Columbus' great discovery.

The rhetorical question Fiske posed to Abby was how all this travel was going to help his history. And the immediate answer was that at last somebody would be able to do justice to Lewis and Clark and their great exploring expedition: "Won't I put some poetry into my account when I get to it? I will make it one of the features of my history." And he concluded, "The brave men who did this on foot deserve to be immortalized. I'll give them their due. I feel it all now and that alone would be worth the trip."

But the history was to profit from something else quite different from the romantic background from which the facts and myths of Lewis and Clark have bequeathed so much to the American national story. From the train window at Pocatello, Idaho, Fiske saw his first wild Indians: "At the station I saw a noble savage, with his squaw and two small sons taking nourishment out of a swill-box! A few braves came capering around on their small horses armed with bows and arrows, and scowled upon us. Anything in human shape so nasty, villainous, and vile must be seen in order to be believed. You wouldn't suppose such hideous and nauseous brutes could be."[17] Since this statement was in a letter to his wife, there was no need for italics to point up his scornful use of the term "noble savage": she knew only too well that the concepts of Rousseau were anathema to her husband. Fiske's knowledge of Indians was firmly based on Francis Parkman who had shown respect and understanding; but Fiske's theories were completely contrary to any romantic ideals of sylvan virtue, and thus he had nothing but scorn for Rousseau and James Fenimore Cooper when it came to red men. While he honestly attempted to give the

Indian his due, Fiske's strong belief was that the red man represented a lower form of society—and at Pocatello he found evidence to prove it. Maintaining the idea of the upward sweep of American destiny, the concept that evolution was a God-designed progressive movement toward higher things, he did not hesitate to insist that "nature red in tooth and claw" not only allowed but aided the weaker forms to decay slowly as the higher forms moved in. Nevertheless, such glimpses as this one did impress upon him the value of ethnological research and brought about in his final history a serious consideration of prehistoric society in America. In truth, this western experience widened Fiske's horizons both for his ultimate good and for his immediate confusion.

The more immediate and unfortunate aspect was to bring to his conscious mind the fact that, after seven years of work, he was not capable of producing a short history; the trip in the West had only served to expand his conception. By mutual agreement with Harpers, the publishing contract was annulled. However, the ultimate good which came from his wider view was the deepening of his whole historical project finally made possible by a remarkable publishing agreement with Henry Houghton of Houghton Mifflin. With this arrangement the pressures of lecturing were to be considerably relieved, and Fiske was to be free to go full-steam ahead with his dream work.

Apparently, Houghton had a true interest in publishing good literature: he was willing to risk something in presenting materials of lasting cultural value. At the same time, he saw John Fiske as a long-term gamble, as a writer whose books would not only add prestige to the firm but eventually pay off financially. The offer he made was most remarkable even under these circumstances. Fiske biographers have variously phrased the terms of the agreement; but, in effect, they placed John on a regular salary so that he would be "placed at ease for the preparation of the fundamental works of his scheme, which required some years of patient research-study." Houghton agreed that, "As it was desirable that the scheme should be kept before the public, Fiske was to have the privilege of lecturing three months of the year on his own account."[18] Nothing was said about any manuscripts which he might produce outside the scheme for the history of the American people. In short, Fiske was at last free to go to work—and equally free to engage in any "moon-lighting" that might appeal to him. By all rules of logic, the lecturing career of John Fiske should at this point have become secondary.

We cannot say positively, however, that it did. From 1889 to 1892 a number of Fiske volumes came from the presses, so there can be no doubt that he managed to do a great deal of writing. Yet, examining carefully what he had outlined in his agreement and measuring it against work actually accomplished up to 1892, we find a goodly portion of the scheme uncompleted. In fact, the final volume for the era of colonization was still not in finished form when Fiske died in 1901; nor did he ever go beyond the Critical Period except for one volume composed of his Civil War lectures. Furthermore, there are a number of volumes issued by other publishers during this time. In noting the long gap in all of his publishing ventures from 1892 to 1894, we see that one of the causes was an increasing demand for his historical lectures and for memorial addresses. We can safely assume that John Fiske's love of good living made it impossible to forgo, as much as perhaps he ought to have done, the financial gains of the lecture circuit. Beyond this economic factor, his was a restless kind of energy that had to be juggling numerous lively projects, constantly playing one off against another.

At the same time, we might also suggest that ever so little Fiske was slowing down. He seems to have had more time at home: a few days of loafing or quiet diversion, a need to refill the wells. Particularly of interest is his work in his conservatory. His own comment shows how firmly his thinking was grounded in ideas related to if not derived from Darwin, Emerson, Thoreau:

[My plants] are far from inanimate substances to me. Indeed, when in their presence I equip my imagination with microscopic power and peer into their simple mechanism. . . . I confess to a peculiar sense of nearness to the profound mystery of existence which surrounds us on every side. And when, in contemplation of this quiet working of immaterial forces, moving without haste, or resting to certain predestined ends, I ask, "Whence this marvellous display of power and purpose?" I feel the answer welling up in the innermost parts of my own being, "Account for yourself and you have accounted for all."[19]

There is an echo here from *Through Nature to God*: "I often think of what Linnaeus said of the unfolding of a blossom: 'I saw God in His glory near me, and bowed my head in worship.' "[20]

Whether abated or unabated, the lecturing to a degree continued. Back in 1872 the Lowell Institute had refused Eliot's suggestion that Fiske be invited there; the funds for the lectures had been specifically designated for speakers who believed in the special divine inspiration of the Scriptures, and John Fiske did not qualify. In 1890 opinion had so far modified that the Lowell Institute invited him to give a series of twelve lectures entitled "The Discovery, Conquest, and Colonization of America." Since Fiske had not in the interim materially altered his religious opinions, he saw this invitation as a vindication of his views and could hardly reject the opportunity.

In the spring of 1892 a golden opportunity arrived: Fiske was asked to be orator at the centennial anniversary of the discovery and naming of the Columbia River. His enchantment with the Far West could not be resisted, and months in advance John worked out a lecture schedule that would take him steadily westward, paying him as he went. In San Francisco he had the great pleasure of meeting John Muir, who did his best to talk Fiske into taking a trip to Alaska.

The centennial celebration itself was the highlight, of course, with excursions on the river, fireworks, banquets, and a host of dignitaries. Before an audience, which included a number of pioneers who had made the trek westward in covered wagons and were now Oregon's white-haired elders, Fiske delivered an address which swept across the narrative of American expansion and ended in a glowing tribute to the natural scenery of Oregon and to her people: "All honor to the sagacious mariner who first sailed upon these waters a century ago! and all honor to the brave pioneers whose labors and sufferings crowned the work! Through long ages to come theirs shall be a sweet and shining memory."[21]

We may not draw conclusions about Fiske's historical writings from this piece which was deliberately designed as oratory and which can be fairly evaluated only against speeches of its own day. Nevertheless, the difference between this lecture and his history is primarily one of tone: if we turn down the volume a little, we still see the strong emphasis on nature and the almost boyish wonder at the stupendous achievement of the pioneers. His whole view of the frontier movement tends to look more backward to Parkman than forward to Frederick Jackson Turner. Our immediate response to such passages as the closing of John Fiske's Oregon speech tells us more about ourselves than about John Fiske or his audience. We catch a glimpse, if we stand aside from ourselves, of what historians mean when they talk about American innocence. For the peroration of Fiske may sound like old, familiar music; but it is indeed a beautiful land, and it was indeed a stupendous achievement—and all our modern sophistication cannot make it less. The sincerity with which he spoke and with which his audience responded removed the possibility of any triteness.

Fiske himself had more than a touch of the explorer. Muir had only confirmed the wisdom of a plan already brewing so that, at the end of his western assignment, Fiske chose to give himself a vacation by making an excursion to Alaska. Once again, we regret that he never seems to have thought of creating a travel book; and, because of the lack of mail service, there are no letters, and the notes in his diaries were never transcribed into a narrative. Futile as it may be, we can imagine that this failure robbed us of what might have been a minor masterpiece of firsthand history. A few notes or references do appear, such as the brief comment in an essay on history in which he describes a painting in an Alaska mission. It was an Adoration of the Magi, and "all the faces—those of the Virgin and Child, of St. Joseph and the Wise Men—were Indian faces."[22] For the most part, when John reached Cambridge in June, he came with a soul full of impressions, a vast collection of photographs, a few brief diary notes, and only one cent in his pocket—the treasures of a true adventurer.

There are few other major lecture experiences to report. A good many of his late appearances on the platform were on memorial occasions like the 250th anniversary of the founding of Middletown in 1900. There had been speeches on the occasions when he received honorary degrees from the University of Pennsylvania as far back as 1894, and doctor of letters and doctor of laws from Harvard about two weeks later. But the last great chapter of this phase of his career was never written, for the capstone would have been his address at the King Alfred Centennial in 1901. He had made great plans for this event and had sketched the general text of what he would say, but John Fiske died a few months before the great occasion.

CHAPTER 5

The Recorded Histories

TO his contemporaries, John Fiske was, I suspect, famous
primarily because of his lectures and only secondarily
because of his written works. Posterity can offer no complete
evaluation of the lecture career since there is no record except
the printed criticisms. We can try to measure the influence and
importance of both phases of his career for his own time, and
we can come to some judgment about the permanent value of
his literary works. If Fiske is to have a place in American letters
(as he has unquestionably earned a place in the life of Victorian
America), that place will be awarded—in my opinion—on his
histories rather than on his philosophical or religious works
which caused so much stir in his own time. Although the philosophical works are vital to the history of ideas and the development of American thought at least on one level, the histories,
despite all their faults, have a greater measure of literary and
esthetic merit.

To appreciate the scope of Fiske's historical writing, the various books should probably be read—like Cooper's Leather-
Stocking tales—in chronological order according to subject.
But, for the picture of Fiske the historian, a good deal is to be
gained by considering them in order of publication, including
both those works intended as part of the panorama and those
incidental to it. In all of these, it is worth repeating, Fiske is
a historian with a thesis: history is the subject matter to prove
the truth of evolution.

Nevertheless, it would be unjust to label these books as tracts
rather than histories, for a survey of the writing of history
shows that he was not the first nor the last to write from a
special point of view. In stating specifically what Fiske believes
his approach to be, he calls his work "scientific history"; but

110

he does not define the term in quite the modern sense. In part, his definition reflects the German scholarship which developed the so-called scientific historian: "It is the business of the historian to inquire into the past experience of the human race. . . . It is a task of exceeding delicacy, and the dispassionate spirit of science is needed for its successful performance. Science does not love or hate its subjects of investigation; the historian must exercise self-control." But, along the way, Fiske inserted a thought which reveals a typical Puritan moral attitude: the historian examines the past "in order to arrive at general views which are correct, in which case they will furnish lessons for the future." And with this note of emphasis he concludes the paragraph: "I do not mean that he should withhold his moral judgment; he will respect intelligence and bow down to virtue, he will expose stupidity and denounce wickedness, wherever he encounters them, but he will not lose sight of the ultimate aim to detect the conditions under which certain kinds of human action thrive or fail; and that is the scientific aim."[1]

Taking this approach of chronology by publication dates and omitting miscellaneous items for encyclopedias and children's books, we go back to the year 1885 when Fiske published *American Political Ideas,* based on the lectures presented five years before at the Royal Institution. (And the Old South Church lectures which had been his initial venture into American history.) As we have noted, he laid the foundations in his work for his interpretation of American history along the lines established in *Cosmic Philosophy.* There, although divorcing himself from the positivist position in philosophy, he had given Comte credit for bringing into prominence the idea of the philosophy of history "which should also be the history of philosophy." Paralleling Comte and Georges Cuvier, Fiske pointed out that, just as the latter found it irrational to study existing organisms without reference to extinct organisms, so the former required that existing opinions be studied in relation to past opinions. In relating the two, Fiske gives a clue to the way in which evolutionists slid over from biology into social fields; but a more important point is his phrasing of the truth which Comte propounded. This truth is the thesis upon which the histories are based: "that each body of doctrines has its root in some ancestral body of doctrines; that throughout the whole of man's speculative career there has been going on an Evolution of Philosophy, of which the thorough recognition of the relativity of knowledge must be the inevitable outcome."[2]

Translating this statement into concrete terms, he focused in *American Political Ideas* on the meaning of the town meeting, traced its origins, showed its relationships to the federal union, and offered his dream of manifest destiny. Whatever strengths and weaknesses his over-all view may have are revealed in this initial volume. And that it had weaknesses cannot be denied: modern critics have been quick to point out its limitations. For example, we have Vernon Parrington's sharp remark that only a New Englander could have betrayed this particular brand of provincialism. On the other hand, the theory led to the development of a pattern which in many respects is one of the values of Fiske's histories. This search for cause and effect, for the ancestral doctrines on which modern doctrines are based, led him into the habit of going deep into the background of any historical period. At times, he spent far too much energy on it and neglected both the middle distance and the foreground. Still, it was a constant reminder of the need to measure American history not in a vacuum but against the backdrop of all Western history if not world history—a reminder which is still valuable to American studies groups of the twentieth century:

The political history of the American people can be rightly understood only when it is studied in connection with that general process of political evolution which has been going on from the earliest times, and of which it is itself one of the most important and remarkable phases. The government of the United States is not the result of special creation but of evolution. . . . So the great political problem which we are (thus far successfully) solving is the very same problem which all civilized peoples have been working upon ever since civilization began. How to insure peaceful concerted action throughout the Whole, without infringing upon local and individual freedom in the Parts. We rate the failure or success of nations politically according to their failure or success in attaining this supreme end.[3]

In applying these general principles, Fiske often had his eye too narrowly fixed on his special thesis of how this evolutionary process worked. The general statement, however, reflects light on Matthew Arnold's view that America had, indeed, solved the political problem. And many of the limitations are more of the era than of Fiske himself, which is evident when we note that Henry Adams comes under fire for similar provincial myopia. (But, of course, Adams too was a New Englander and a Harvard professor.) Had the process been as scientific as Fiske supposed it to be, he would not have been led into prophecies as grimly amusing as history has made them. To Fiske, the world was to become thoroughly Anglo-Americanized, led by these two nations to Tennyson's "parliament of man and the federation of the world," or to the point of "peaceful concerted action throughout the Whole."

From his lectures he again drew a literary work in 1888, *The Critical Period of American History*, a detailed examination of the years between 1782 and 1789, and one designed to reflect the importance of the slow growth of the concept of a constitutional federal government whose powers superseded those of the several states—the foundation, in other words, of the concept of government sorely tested during the Civil War. And Fiske's contention is that the United States narrowly averted disaster during these years. Perhaps the thesis that these were years of crisis in many senses as well as critical in the various steps in the growth of governmental patterns contains errors, seen from retrospect. The thesis has attracted a good deal of scholarly attention, and it has been equally refuted and defended; this is possible because, like a great proportion of Fiske's theoretical work, the broader aspects are so wide as to make application almost free-wheeling, while a careful study of primary sources can easily prove errors against him on a concrete level. But there is in it an echo of the ideas in Lincoln's Gettysburg Address. Nor is it surprising that the thesis should find approval from a generation which had fought the Civil War.

The story of these years could scarcely be told, of course, without reference to the Constitutional Convention, Shays' Rebellion, and paper money. But Fiske found all of these particularly intriguing to deal with: the convention gave him the opportunity to put forth the Connecticut Compromise with a kind word for the constitution of his native state; the second had touched upon the history of Petersham; and paper money was one of the panaceas he loved to attack. All such material was grist to support the theory, as was the problem of tariff and free trade which he assaulted vigorously with his usual argument that tariffs did nothing but interfere with the true course of evolution.

There are, however, two notes which are quite aside from the general evolutionary theory. First, he was well aware of the vital role played by transportation and communication. While he does mention the steamboat, he says nothing about roads or canals. However, remembering boyhood discussions in Middletown, he makes a point of the importance of the railroads in the development of the country. Without them and the telegraph, the distance between Oregon, for example, and Washington D.C., would have been all but insurmountable. And the Civil War would have been nearly impossible militarily. Second, more in concern for problems of his own day but apropos of the system of checks and balances, he comes down strongly on the tyranny of democracy. It is a great relief to him to know that the independence of the executive branch can protect us "from the knavery and folly of our representatives." Finally, he relates the idea back to evolutionary concepts with the comment: "Such are the vicissitudes of peril which society must pass through on its way toward that liberty of which eternal vigilance is the price!"[4] True liberty can be earned only after long years of struggle; before that we cannot say that the political problem is forever solved.

Perhaps the first full-blown history, after all, is *The Beginnings of New England,* essentially an expansion and a careful illustration of the thesis in *American Political Ideas.* Fiske opens in his customary fashion with a long prefatory chapter, "The Roman Idea and the English Idea," in which he sees three major approaches used by a people in taking over a territory: the oriental idea, conquest without incorporation; the Roman idea, conquest with incorporation; and the English idea, conquest with representation. From this basis he moves on to how vital Puritanism was in keeping alive the last of these approaches which, it scarcely needs to be added, is the highest yet evolved. The Puritan theology as it created certain philosophical and political ways of thinking is then proved to be the deciding thread in the growth of New England.

In the major portion of his book, he narrates events in New England down to 1689 with the conclusion that the seeds of 1776 were already planted by that time. Fiske's belief in the slow, painful process of evolution, which for him is Divine plan, is revealed by such comments as "we realize the import of saying that in the sight of the Lord a thousand years are but as a day, and we feel that the work of the Lord cannot be done by the listless or the slothful," and "God never meant that in this fair but treacherous world in which he has placed us we should earn our salvation without steadfast labor."[5]

There is unquestionably a variation of the old doctrine of predestination in his view of evolution: "The philosophic student of history often has occasion to see how God is wiser than man. . . . It is part of the irony of human destiny that the end we really accomplish by striving with might and main is apt to be something quite different from the end we dreamed of as we started on our arduous labour."[6] Such an observation makes clear what Fiske means when he says, in his portrait of Calvin, that "His theology had much in it that is in striking harmony with modern scientific philosophy, and much in it, too, that the descendants of his Puritan converts have learned to loathe as sheer diabolism."[7]

Along the way, Fiske takes an occasional sideswipe at certain events in his own day; these, too, reflect the belief in the inevitable process. More concretely, they reflect a predilection for laissez faire policies as being the soundest method for letting the process work itself out. This explanation, at least, is the theoretical one. Beneath it, one detects a solid basis of old-fashioned New England politics: the indigent have only themselves to blame, and anything that even remotely smacks of the welfare state interferes with the proper growth of moral character. Fiske's scientific theories are so thoroughly intertwined with the ethics and morality of the Connecticut variation of Puritanism that they are completely inseparable. More often than not, the scientific theories are but modernized ways of explaining old beliefs.

Thus, having noted that historians have found the vitality of the Roman system impaired by the "false political economy which taxes all for the benefit of the few," by the debauching view which regards civil office as "private perquisite and not public trust," and most painful of all, "by the communistic practice of feeding an idle proletariat out of the imperial treasury," he adds: "The names of these deadly social evils are not un-

familiar to American ears. Even of the last we have heard
ominous whispers in the shape of bills to promote mendicancy
under the specious guise of fostering education or rewarding
military service."[8] And his attitude is even more sharply underlined by, "As President Cleveland has well said, it is not the
business of a government to support its people, but of the people
to support their government; and once to lose sight of this vital
truth is as dangerous as to trifle with some stealthy narcotic
poison."[9]

No one today wants to quarrel with objections to much of
Fiske's work even in this notable volume. In the long run, these
weaknesses may weigh in the balance against him; but, at least
for the moment, there is reason for a sober pause of consideration
of what he has to say about Puritanism, the main subject
of the book. In the revolt of the early twentieth century against
moral standards that were unrealistically strict, we have too
easily made whipping boys of our Puritan ancestors. American
innocence—or ignorance—was the result of a narrow view. It
impeded not only our moral but our esthetic and cultural
sophistication. We had a long, hard labor to recover from the
inhibitions inflicted by our Puritan background. It is refreshing
to be reminded that perhaps after all we owe a debt to the same
background for the very political, even spiritual, way of life
that makes America what it is. And whatever price may be paid
in provincialism, a Connecticut Yankee (by virtue of Connecticut
freedom from theocracy) stands in a rather good position to
give us that reminder.

Fiske, of course, would not have been concerned with the
strictness of Puritan moral standards: to the proper Victorian,
it was all to the good. If not here, he does elsewhere thoroughly
appreciate the damages done by the esthetic limitations of
Puritanism. But his emphasis is on the contrast of the dogmatic
theocracy with individual religious and political theory. Nevertheless, his basic demonstration that these were but obverse
sides of the same coin is applicable to all phases of Puritan
background. Concretely he points up the solid, common-sense,
middle-class practicality of the Puritan approach to matters of
this world. And, in insisting on the diversity as well as on the
homogeneity of what we loosely call "Puritans," he sets off
beautifully balanced portraits of such diverse figures as William

Bradford, Roger Williams, and Thomas Hooker. We need not consent to the overriding theory in order to profit from these individual perceptions or to enjoy the narrative.

Pushed to its extreme, the theory says that English Puritanism, descendant from Teutonic institutions, was the major factor in the growth of New England and hence of the United States. John Fiske does not push it to this extreme, despite what his critics say; he may, however, overplay his hand. But we have only to imagine, as he suggests, what a different history would have been written if France, instead of the English burgher class, had won control of the new continent. A careful review of the new histories which are examining the differences between Canada and the United States might reveal that John Fiske wrote better than we have so far been willing to admit.

When Fiske first became aware that his concept of American history would not fit into the plan he had bargained for with Harpers, he saw his expanded view as composed of three parts: "the sifting of the nations for the germs of the new order of political organization based upon the inalienable rights of man; the planting of thèse germs in the new world of America, and their political integration; and their fruitage in the federal government of the United States." In this phrasing, his basic theories show strongly; but, by the time he discussed the project with Houghton, he had developed a more concrete outline, one closer to the facts of history itself. The new scheme had five divisions: "the Epoch of American Discovery; the Period of Colonization; the Revolutionary War; the Critical Period; the establishment of the Federal Government of the United States and its development."[10] One other phase besides the New England colonies which was easy to prepare was a revision of the lecture course on the Revolutionary War. While both of these were being compiled from materials already prepared, Fiske turned his attention to the first division, the period of discovery.

Never one to place all his eggs in one basket, at the same time he was developing a book to be called *Civil Government in the United States,* a work designed as both a possible textbook for schools and information for the general reader. Obviously, this book was a reworking of the materials he had already used both in his lectures and his writings. Its central idea was, of course, the thesis that the town meeting is the foundation for our federal government. The resulting volume was published in 1890 with some suggestive Questions and Directions at the end of each chapter. These trimmings were prepared by Mr. F. A. Hill, headmaster of the Cambridge English School. With this book now on the market, Fiske returned to his efforts on the age of discovery.

The major narrative events in this three-volume work are too well known to need restatement here. For his analysis of these events, Fiske chose, or saw as most accurate, the intermingled themes of the European world of Columbus' time and the American world, both North and South, that lay virtually unknown to the West. A good portion of the first volume is devoted to the Western Hemisphere before 1492 and is strongly flavored with Spencerian sociology. Setting aside for a moment any debate about theory, we note that Fiske was remarkably alert to the need for Indian studies and to men whom posterity has singled out as leaders in the field. Anyone could have seen, of course, that the theme of the vanishing red man was no mere romantic notion; but few scholars pointed out the importance of capturing what knowledge could still be learned. "It is important that no time be lost in gathering and putting on record all that can be learned of the speech and arts, the customs and beliefs, everything that goes into the philology and anthropology of the red men."[11] And he singles out the excellent effort by Major Powell and George Catlin as illustrations of the high quality of some of the studies being done, surely most perceptive choices. John Fiske was not the last to wish that more support had been given to Major Powell.

For us today one of the most striking, though not particularly significant, minor statements is Fiske's distinction between the Northmen and Columbus. Indeed, because of his fascination with Icelandic literature, he gives an inordinate amount of space to the whole question. Still it was an initial step essential to proving his dramatic statement which ten years of study had confirmed, "The voyage of Columbus was the most important event in human history since the birth of Christ." He does not even challenge the voyages of the Northmen, but he maintains that "to speak to them as constituting in any legitimate use of the phrase as a Discovery of America is simply absurd." Greenland was regarded as part of the European world, and America in the summer of 1492 "needed to be discovered as much as if Leif Ericson or the whole race of Northmen had never existed." Measuring the voyages of the Scandinavians against the effects on both worlds, he finds no effect on Europe except for the scanty but interesting record in Icelandic literature and, in the Western Hemisphere, no effect beyond "cutting down a few trees and killing a few Indians."

And he underlines the idea: "In the outlying world of Greenland, it is not improbable that the blood of the Eskimos may have received some slight Scandinavian infusion. But upon the aboriginal world of the red men, from Davis Strait to Cape Horn, it is not likely that any impress of any sort was ever made." And, if any antiquarians wish to offer the tower at Newport, Rhode Island, as evidence to the contrary, Fiske calmly refers to that as Governor Arnold's old mill. Therefore, while it is true that Leif Ericson and his friends made voyages to what we now know as the coast of America, "it is an abuse of language to say that they 'discovered' America. In no sense was any real contact established between the eastern and the western hemispheres until the great voyage of Columbus in 1492."[12]

Fiske must have had a most enjoyable time writing these volumes. There is a zest, a lively tension throughout that keeps the reader's attention. And this tone makes it evident that the occasional bits of humor are not pasted in for the purpose of popularizing. John Fiske's humor is never subtle, but usually playful and mild; and it appears only when he feels himself sufficiently in command to relax with his readers. Here it appears for the most part in lightly entertaining footnotes. Quoting a book which he used for source material on Indians, Fiske writes that the author said of matriarchal societies: "With the woman rests the security of the marriage ties" and "she rarely abuses the privilege; that is, she never sends her husband 'to the home of his fathers' unless he richly deserves it." And John asks, "Should not Mr. Cushing have said 'home of his mothers' or perhaps of 'his sisters and his cousins and his aunts'?"[13] A little later he makes a dry criticism of Prescott, not one of his favorite historians. Having written that "there were occasions when the Aztecs tortured their prisoners before sending them to the altar," he adds in a footnote: "Mr. Prescott, to avoid shocking the reader with details, refers him to the twenty-first canto of Dante's inferno."[14] All of which is perhaps not vital nor particularly historical, but it does convey the flavor of Fiske's writing when he is at his most benign. At brief moments and wide intervals, he resembles a shaggy puppy at play.

Here, as elsewhere, Fiske's scholarship is broader than it is deep. He read widely and borrowed heavily—and often from secondary and tertiary sources. In his considerations of Columbus, for instance, he wisely depended on Las Casas; but, at the same time, he leaned strongly on Washington Irving and George Bancroft. And it is much to be doubted that even his most devoted followers can argue for much originality of research or thesis. The evolutionary view of history was propounded by a number of others, including Sir Henry Maine and Edward Freeman; but no one else had so thoroughly and consistently made a synthesis of the American story. Irving had written the life of Columbus; Prescott, the conquest of Mexico and Peru; and others had concerned themselves with other aspects; but Fiske swept the whole canvas. The cosmic view has its faults, but it does capture something of the vastness; it does emphasize the interlocking of cause and effect. In ranging as he did across the background of history, John Fiske brought out for a wide audience, though he certainly did not invent, what we might call the "need for a consciousness of cultural ecology," the awareness of the total environment. The evolutionary historians are now out of favor; but, transformed as it may be, this aspect of their work is basic to our modern understanding of our world.

There now remained but one phase of Fiske's work to bring him to the era covered by *The Critical Period* and to round out the first four divisions of his project: the age of colonization had been treated only through New England and only to 1689, and the task of examining the Middle Atlantic area and the South lay before him. Before publication of volumes to fill the gap, there came another of the long pauses which we have come to expect. Other projects included a trip to the Northwest, a life of Youmans, and a history of the United States for schools. Each of these projects can be defended as a legitimate interruption. The life of Youmans, for example, had been promised and fulfilled a debt to a man who had done much for Fiske's early career. And each in its own way adds to the portrait of the man

Fiske as he was, not as he ought to have been (that is, if he truly desired to be recorded by the future as a great historian); but, whatever its value, each was an interruption to the work that he himself considered his great scheme. These works had no direct bearing on the history, but they do require that the biographer sketch in a few lines of his portrait suggesting that John Fiske himself often stood in the way of the literary career he had dreamed about fully as much as circumstances or external events may have done.

The rounding out of the colonial period was slowly accomplished in the next few years with *Old Virginia and Her Neighbors,* published in 1879, and *The Dutch and Quaker Colonies in America,* published in 1889. Fiske added a third volume in some respects rather unusual and at the same time not surprising in view of his scope and his friendship with Parkman. *New France and New England,* which was published after his death in 1901, rounded out the story of the New England colonies as well as that of New York. It might also be said to be the volume that drew together the themes of all of the stories of all of the colonies.

In the first two volumes, like his compatriot Henry Adams, Fiske has been charged with being too provincial, too New England. All things considered, there may be some justice in the accusation; it should, however, be charged against the theory about town meetings rather than against regional narrowness. Carried away by his thesis, he sometimes tended to see other colonies in terms of the same religious homogeneity which characterized New England. Possibly one can almost make this work with the southern colonies—though certainly Virginia would resent being looked upon as "Massachusetts in a warmer climate." And no analysis of this area can be complete without recognition of the difference between the Tidewater and the Scotch-Irish back countries, nor of the strong Catholic influence in Maryland and Georgia. Fiske was well aware of these differences and dwelt upon them to a reasonable degree.

Critics insist, however, that this very diversity threw him off when he came to the Middle Colonies, for he tried to prove that the lack of Puritan background slowed down the democratic process in these colonies. Henry Adams saw more clearly when he pointed out that Pennsylvania with its heterogeneous groups and its tradition of religious tolerance was far in advance in accepting and developing the national interests. Both New England and the South remained regional in many aspects for a much longer time. Nevertheless, this criticism of Fiske cannot be accepted without reservations; the critics were sometimes as guilty of jumping to grand conclusions as Fiske himself was. The various details they complain of his having failed to comprehend are often stated explicitly, but they may easily be overlooked since the focus is on the idea that English Puritanism can be proved to be the source of the American political idea as it developed in all of the colonies. Yet, even in the theory, Fiske held to diversity in unity and had repeatedly emphasized the heterogeneous facets in New England itself; often it is the critics who ride the thesis harder than the writer himself. Had Fiske gone on to write of a period of history which included the West, the charge of provincialism would have been harder to support. Through personal experience Fiske knew the West and her history was in his consciousness—as remarks in various essays indicate. The South had not been made so directly vivid to him.

Furthermore, with the southern colonies, it is the scope of the work which may be held largely responsible for its weaknesses (though not for individual errors in facts). The introduction contains a *caveat* which carping critics deemphasize, for John clearly states that he has not labeled the work a history of the southern colonies since this is not within his purpose: "My aim is to follow the main stream of causation from the time of Raleigh to the time of Dinwiddie, from its sources down to its absorption in the mightier stream." Possibly it is true that the result is the same; yet a writer is entitled to be judged in terms of what he attempts rather than of what somebody thinks he ought to have done. By opening with Sir Francis Drake and Richard Hakluyt, Fiske immediately proves just how completely his theme is going to dominate. And this theme makes it necessary to give much space to the ages of Elizabeth I and James I to the neglect of the detailed history of some of the colonies themselves. Partly, too, the dates within which Fiske chooses to work allow Virginia the bulk of two volumes while Maryland receives 125 pages, the Carolinas only 80, and Georgia a mere mention. This count, Fiske's own, is given as a part of the explanation in his preface.

Several of the characteristic themes and tones reappear. Following his own concept that each age must be measured by its own terms, he can find no cause for holding an earlier period responsible for slavery. The Elizabethans thought nothing of the practice: it was, in fact, a kind deed to rescue Negroes from barbarity and carry them off to a Christian country where their bodies might be clothed and their souls prepared for heaven. But Fiske observed that he found this doctrine less acceptable in his own age, three centuries later, when he heard the same defense preached from a Connecticut pulpit: "It takes men a weary while to learn the wickedness of anything that puts gold in their purses."[15] The note of humor also flashes forth upon occasion, as when he reports that Captain Philip Amadas and Captain Arthur Barlowe returned to England and said that they had visited Wingandacoa; "but the queen, with a touch of the euphuism then so fashionable, suggested that it should be called, in honour of herself, Virginia."[16] Still, he admired Elizabeth immensely; but he could not abide her successor, "a quaint pedantic little Scotchman, with uncouth figure and shambling gait and a thickness of utterance partly due to an ill-formed tongue and partly to an excessive indulgence in mountain dew, had stepped into her place."[17]

Throughout the history, we see the ever-present interest in the growth and development of political institutions and the implications of evolution that Fiske reads into this development. "In the unfolding of these events there is a poetic beauty and grandeur as the purpose of the infinite wisdom reveals itself in its cosmic process, slowly but inexorably, hasting not but resting not, heedless of the clashing aims and discordant cries of shortsighted mortals, sweeping their tiny efforts into its majestic current, and making all contribute to the fulfillment of God's will."[18]

A most interesting case study can be used to illustrate the picture of Fiske and his critics. The publication of *The Dutch and Quaker Colonies in America* was followed up by a review in the *North American Review*. In her article, Mrs. Van Rensellaer sets forth a wonderful example of the points of difference. As we might expect, she opens with a modified version of the provincial charge; she had hoped much from Mr. Fiske for many reasons, among which was the fact that "he has shown much less narrowness of vision in dealing with New England than some of her other sons."[19] But she seems not to have noticed that Fiske quite agreed with her in this attitude. Early in the second chapter, which is entirely devoted to early Dutch influences upon England, he underlines the fact that earlier writers on American history failed to give due consideration to the contributions of non-English peoples to American civilization. "Perhaps this may have been because our earliest historians were men of New England whose attention was unduly occupied with their own neighborhood."[20] And Fiske tried quite seriously to evaluate the non-English contributions; yet his thesis is ever before him: "If we ask why England has been preeminent as a colonizer, we may call attention to the fact that nearly all of the free constitutions of the world have been consciously copied from England or from the United States during the nineteenth century. Between these two facts the connection is far from accidental."[21]

In charging Fiske with carelessness in the use of source materials, Mrs. Van Rensellaer quite thoroughly proves her point by citing chapter and verse. Especially when she singles out the uses of Irving's *Knickerbocker History*, we cannot help but agree that she is correct. From Irving's work he quotes heavily; and, for all that he indicates that he is aware of Irving's burlesque, he does not seem to keep this factor in mind. It may well be that a large borrowing from *Knickerbocker* is a deliberate part of the attempt to create a wide audience appeal, to keep the tone from becoming too heavy; but there are times when Fiske takes Deidrich seriously or permits his readers to do so. The fact is that Fiske was fond of using literary sources; for, as an avid reader of Dickens, Scott, and George Eliot, he liked to turn to the creative writers and often found them closer to the truth than those he called the "dry-as-dust historians." While he did not hesitate to criticize the poet who was inaccurate, as he felt Longfellow was in his *Hiawatha*, he could still say that he had "known the conscientious poet to set public opinion right on a matter of history."[22] His example is also his good neighbor Longfellow, who took the trouble to dig back into the records to correct the interpretation of the role played by Cotton Mather in the Salem witchcraft trials.

The two-volume *Dutch and Quaker Colonies* closes with: "In the cosmopolitanism which showed itself so early in New Amsterdam and has ever since been fully maintained, there was added to the American national life the variety, the flexibility, the generous breadth of view, the spirit of compromise and conciliation needful to save the nation from rigid provincialism. Among the circumstances which prepared the way for a rich and varied American nation, the preliminary settlement of the geographical center of the country by Dutchmen was certainly one of the most fortunate."[23] Mrs. Van Rensellaer, who quotes this passage, adds: "These are intelligent words, and the story of New York, if intelligently told, would amply prove them such; but Mr. Fiske's readers may not unnaturally wonder why he wrote them."[24]

The last part of this statement is sharply unjust; nevertheless, the book is so written that her charge cannot simply be thrown out of court. And, in the final analysis, she pins down fairly accurately the reason for the disagreement: "his tendency to make the political condition of a community the sole test of its temper, its ideals, and its social state in the broad meaning of the term. . . . He identifies the love and enjoyment of liberty too closely with the character of current political institutions."[25] It is precisely this emphasis rather than too great an insistence on homogeneity which is at fault; variety and flexibility were vital to evolution, and more than once Fiske pointed out that it was the sport or variation that became the basis for further advance.

Turning to his study of Pennsylvania, Fiske began with a broad background portrait of William Penn and his travels in Germany. He did so to develop the theme of Quaker struggles against religious persecution, and it leads to a tribute to the tolerance of Penn's colony. For Fiske, toleration sounds a note which echoes throughout his thinking, a note which is often overlooked by those who find him too insistent on homogeneity. Religious tolerance has always been high on Fiske's list of approved virtues—and for very personal reasons; but we must not overlook the fact that it ties in with his scientific theory very closely.[26]

As Fiske had pointed out before in commenting on the Spanish Inquisition and on the persecution of Huguenots by the French government, persecution for religious reasons interferes with the process of natural selection. "The evolution of a higher civilization can best be attained by allowing to individual tastes, impulses, and capacities the freest possible play."[27] As he says, a wise horticulturist nurtures many an aberrant plant; and a race of "self-reliant, inventive, and enterprising Yankees" is not produced by winnowing out all of the men and women bold and bright enough to do their own thinking. In short, it is likely to be those who prove most adaptable to environment and thus to continuing the evolutionary process, who are also religious skeptics. This, of course, is underlined by the religious as well as the scientific value of tolerance: religion is a matter between the individual soul and its God, and only by complete individual freedom to search for truth can higher truths be discovered and revealed.

Fiske's treatment of William Penn and the political situation in the colony comes as close as any passage in his writing to demonstrating the extent to which he was himself a man of the people. Granting that Penn was remarkably democratic in his thinking, Fiske feels that Penn nevertheless regarded himself "as a kind of patriarch who knew much better what was good for his little sylvan community than the people themselves. In this assumption he was very likely correct." In explanation, Fiske adds caustically, "but it is one of the essential features of a thorough-going democracy that those who do not know what is best should have a much greater part in government than those who do, since they are much more numerous." The concept that "one man is as good as another" is a colossal untruth; in reality, democracy rests "on the ubiquitous fact that all men are directly interested in good government, while its successes have often been due to the practical recognition of the truth that some men are born to lead and others to follow." And William Penn was obviously a born leader—and, for the most part, his colonists had sense enough to realize this fact. Or, as Fiske puts it in a foot-note: "Why, Patrick," exclaims the landlord whose mind is dallying with Bentonian ideas, "isn't one man as good as another?" "Faith, he is, your honour, and a d——d sight better!"[28]

The treatment may be brief, but there is time—as there was

also in the volume on Virginia—to comment on the Scotch-Irish. The influence of this group is a theme which was first suggested to him by the work of John Ropes, and Fiske had looked into it rather carefully during his studies in Britain back in the 1880's. What he drew from this examination was the idea that since Scotch-Irish Presbyterians had been forced by experience in Ulster to keep church and state separate, they, as emigrants to the new world, were liberal and tolerant in principle. Thus, in spite of their rigid theology, they were able to harmonize with the neighboring German groups—Lutherans, Mennonites, Dunkers.

A partial union of these two great streams of immigration, the Ulster and the Palatinate, swept across the South; "it influenced South Carolina and Maryland powerfully, completely renovated society in North Carolina, and broke down the sway of the Cavalier aristocracy in Virginia." This group, Fiske writes, not only remade the South but also raised Pennsylvania to third place in population by 1770; and it formed the bulk of pioneers moving into Kentucky, Tennessee, and ultimately the entire Mississippi Valley. "In all these directions . . . this sturdy population, distilled through the Pennsylvania alembic, has formed the main strength of American democracy, and its influence on American life has been manifold."[29] Had Fiske continued his story to include the westward movement, it is a safe conjecture that the treatment of the theme of diversity would have grown as that of homogeneity faded.

In a number of ways there is a distinct falling off in these two books as if they had been written somewhat in haste. Too often a chapter is labeled, like those in eighteenth-century novels, "How so and so came to pass," or "In which such and such takes place." And Fiske too often uses the threadbare device of winding up a chapter by writing, "but this is a story for a new chapter." The principle that history should be presented as narrative is sound enough—it certainly makes for both good lecturing and lively reading—but it should not be driven to the point of adopting weary conventions from fiction. These stylistic devices can possibly be attributed to haste or impetuous writing, but more basic weaknesses can partly be explained by insistence on the thesis; for so firmly did Fiske see things from the point of view of his theory that he lacked the objectivity to see how completely he was bending fact to meet theory rather than using theory to interpret fact.

This explanation is only a guess, for there may also have been a more elusive and subtle reason. The rising urban America of the 1890's did not seem to be moving in the direction Fiske had predicted, the Spanish-American War hardly suggested the evolutionary advance of an enlightened people, and vast hordes of immigrants threatened to inundate the process. Elsewhere he had stated that the cheapness and ease of travel had done much to make America the dumping ground for a much worse class of immigrants from all quarters. He feared that it would be difficult, if not impossible, to assimilate them and teach them American political ideas with sufficient rapidity.[30] Although Fiske had not abandoned the approval of variety and flexibility, these people were not the boldest and brightest ones. Too much in the world of the *fin de siècle* was out of step for it all to be smoothed away by talking in terms of long-range results. Whether deep inside John Fiske found his confidence shaken, we can never know. We have seen that the religious note became stronger in the philosophical writings from the 1880's onward. That he must have felt, subconsciously at least, that all was not well we can fairly safely surmise. The typical Victorian response, the typical human response, is to trumpet more loudly: the less certain one is, the less willing to give ground. This tendency would be reinforced by the role of teacher and guide that John Fiske had played for so many years.

In a curious sense, he was on the very edge of a position in which he had so many years before placed his old minister, the Reverend Jeremiah Taylor. A few more years and Fiske would have found himself begging the young not to abandon the beliefs of the fathers, not to pursue the false new gods. Finally, of course, we who come after William James can nod wisely and remind Fiske that there is never Truth, only truths. The truth of Pennsylvania history may not be that of Connecticut history, and the reality of United States history must somehow square with them both. One theory, unless it be so broad as to be meaningless, cannot cover all.

But, if these pressures were in effect during the preparation of these particular volumes, Fiske apparently overcame, or came to terms with, them as he put together the materials for *New*

France and New England. Though an uncompleted book, it captures some of the earlier enchantment of style. The idea behind the book, or the idea of including it in the series, is in a way not remarkable. Those chapters of American history dealing with the French and Indian War, the long struggle between the two powers, cannot possibly be overlooked if the picture is to be complete. In all probability the idea of placing this material in a separate volume was the direct and natural result of Fiske's theory. Only by dealing with Spanish Florida and the Southwest could he have found other means of demonstrating so clearly the contrast between an English colony and the others. But France had long been his classical example of contemporary modifications of what he called the Roman method of colonization, the approach used by absolute monarchy. Also, it is true that France fits the facts of our history—the power of Spain died out too early; and the struggle in North America was indeed between France and England. Furthermore, there is a point in Fiske's contrast between the more or less independent colonies of Great Britain and the overprotected, overlegislated attempts of the French king, a contrast which reveals itself in the present-day history of French Canada to point up the differences between us and America's northern neighbor. I do not mean to suggest that we can draw upon the New England town-meeting idea or any of the detailed aspects of John Fiske's theory to explain history, but his underlying principles serve to focus on points often neglected.

As for the book itself, Fiske was in the process of revising it when he died. No real evaluation can justly be made without a knowledge of what he intended it to be. Keeping this in mind, and regarding it as an incomplete work though more than a draft, we can note some aspects of his work which might not show so visibly in a completed task. Possibly most noticeable is his method of placing various related lectures side by side and interweaving them into a rounded narrative. *New France and New England,* which breaks rather obviously into these lecture portions, begins with a long tale of French explorations and attempts at colonization from the voyages of Norman sailors in the days of Francis I through Jacques Cartier to the death of La Salle. Immediately after this discussion is a very good but unrelated chapter on the witchcraft period in Salem and one

on the Great Awakening. The rest is a detailed narrative of the
events from Louisbourg to the fall of Quebec. These fragments
are a solid reminder of the basic lecture approach behind all of
Fiske's books. The earliest chapter demonstrates strongly the
way he made use of source materials: as it stands, it pays
tribute by its heavy borrowing to the great work of Francis
Parkman. Since this portion was supposedly all but finished, it
is doubtful that Fiske would have done much to make it more
his own—the work of other historians was more than once woven
in without apology when it met with his needs and his approval.

We always come to the end of a discussion of this nature with
a handful of miscellaneous leftovers. The story has been told,
the curtain should come down; but, above all, Fiske was not a
tidy or orderly man; or at least, in working out his projects,
his orderliness was not of the pigeonhole or filing-cabinet
variety. In 1900 he again interrupted his history to prepare for
publication of his Civil War lectures in a volume called *The
Mississippi Valley in the Civil War*. Among his notes and papers
were the beginnings of what would have been additional volumes
in the grand project; the next step was to work out the interpretation of the early years of the republic which would show the
military society gradually giving way to the industrial.

Through the years there had also been other books, mostly
collections of essays, lectures, and articles. There had been
who knows how many pages passing across his desk and ranging
from hackwork and potboilers to minor masterpieces. I have
not attempted an exhaustive presentation of all of Fiske's writings: he was too prolific and too repetitious. As a historian or
a literary figure, a man should be allowed at last to stand on
his best works; for the rest are of value only as they tell us
something of the best or of the man himself. If this suggestion
be accepted, there is nothing more that needs to be listed or
discussed.

In the spring of 1901 began the elaborate and arduous task
of remodeling Mrs. Stoughton's house in Cambridge into the
Fiske family homestead. John's mother was putting her house
in order; the family was to move in with her and take over the
house when she died. For Fiske, this change meant, of course,
organizing his own household—and particularly the library—
for the move. Worn out by these chores and by the heat of late

June, Fiske was advised by his physician to take a sea trip. With his son Herbert he sailed to Gloucester and died there quite peacefully on July 4. He is buried, of course, in Petersham. Hosmer reports, and the story is probably not apochryphal, that Fiske had once calmly observed that death was but going to Petersham to stay—and so apparently it was. The huge stone over his grave is rather too allegorical for modern taste, but it bears the motto which Fiske would have found most satisfactory. He had first discovered it under a little picture, later had it worked into the paneling over his fireplace, and now he rested beneath it eternally: *Disce ut semper victurus, vive ut cras moriturus.*

CHAPTER 6

A Backward Glance

I *Contemporary Reputation*

AT the time of his death in 1901 John Fiske was a great man. For many years his essays had commanded attention in the major periodicals, both in the United States and in England. His books were reviewed and often praised by men of stature. Young people bent on literary careers sought him out for advice, and universities gave him honorary degrees. There were reservations, of course, but it was not a small chorus of voices that hailed him as the greatest philosopher and historian America had yet given the world; and men whose critical judgment commanded respect predicted that Fiske had earned a permanent and prominent place in the American Hall of Fame.

Eulogies are always to be taken with more than one grain of salt; yet, when properly salted down, they do help bring into focus the portrait of the man. Something can be learned from the tone: whether it is highly or even overly laudatory, or whether it damns with faint praise. But more, if we can make a montage or composite photograph of what the eulogies say, we begin to see the qualities or characteristics which seemed to mark the man for distinction as an individual among his contemporaries. Curiously enough, the note about Fiske which is struck over and over again is the dual, and for us contradictory, role of scholar and commoner. John Spencer Clark repeatedly echoes this theme:

Had he produced his historic work in the quiet retirement of his library, we should have had unquestionably a fine, scholarly performance; but would it possibly have been wanting in those strong, humanistic characteristics which pervade all of his historic writing,— the evidence that during the whole period of his historic composition he was in close touch with the common people. . . .

Then, too, he derived much pleasure and inspiration from being brought into close contact with the masses of his countrymen through the lecture platform. He was a true democrat of the Jeffersonian and Lincoln stamp, and thoroughly believed in the good sense of the people as a whole. . . .[1]

Brother-in-law James Brooks, speaking at the Sesquicentennial Petersham Anniversary, emphasizes the scholar by always referring to John as Dr. Fiske; but what he most emphasizes is the common touch:

"The Idea of God" and "The Destiny of Man" . . . are part of the history of Petersham because they are the germ of all history and all biography. . . . They determine for the ploughman in his furrow, for the smith at his forge, for the statesman in the halls of legislature, and for the judge upon the bench, as well as for the minister at the altar, what he is and ought to be and do.[2]

The very fact that Elbert Hubbard joined the ranks in 1905 attests to Fiske's common appeal. With a typical bourgeois approach, Hubbard overemphasizes Fiske's precocity and great learning; but he, too, focuses on the popular level: "John Fiske made the science of Darwin and Wallace palatable to orthodox theology, and it is to the earnest and eloquent words of Fiske that we owe it that Evolution is taught everywhere in the public schools and even in sectarian colleges in America."[3]

But not always are the two roles together. The heaviest objections came from those who questioned Fiske's scholarship. And, even in his lifetime, there were many who praised the popularizer while implying that this was Fiske's only true merit. As early as 1911, his colleague Professor James K. Hosmer reiterated Fiske's philosophical greatness and attacked the view which lessened his stature. Hosmer resented the picture of Fiske as a mere popularizer "whose merit lies solely, or for the most part, in the fact that while appropriating materials accumulated by others, he had only Goldsmith's faculty of rendering them graceful and attractive to the mass of readers." In this quick comment, and the following paragraph, Hosmer comes as close as anyone to assessing the basic qualities of a Fiske portrait: "In a high sense he was indeed a popularizer. He wore upon himself like an ample garment a splendid erudition under which he moved, however, not at all oppressed or trammelled. Much of the lore of Greece, Rome, the orient, and also modern peoples was as familiar to him as the contents of the morning papers. With acumen he selected, and his memory retained; and the cells of his capacious brain held it ready for instant use."[4]

Actually, those who would combine scholar and commoner tell us as much about the age as about John Fiske. Phrases relating to the "people" are used in two senses, and Fiske's contemporaries often fail to discriminate between the two. One use of the "common people" designates those who attended Fiske's lectures, largely the educated middle class, the same group for whom the magazines in which his work appeared were designed. The other use is directed toward lesser folk, usually rural; and it is both sentimentalized and romanticized. However, various events from Fiske's life and his own words from a number of sources demonstrate that he was not sympathetic to the masses. James Brooks' smith at the forge was Longfellow's Village Blacksmith, not Edwin Markham's Man With the Hoe. Farmers who came to hear Fiske's lectures were envisioned as embryo Lincolns learning by the light of the fire. Omitting comments on the commune aspects, the combination of study and work at Brook Farm would fit well the picture in the minds of those who related scholar and commoner in one man.

The philosophic or esthetic concept that the child and the common man were close to nature and therefore in tune with universal truth still held—though Fiske himself might have been inclined to question it; and there was yet no disillusionment with Jefferson's belief that education would lift and ennoble the ordinary human being. This portrait of Fiske assumed the possibility that also inspired Whitman in his image of himself as the poet of democracy. Only for an age which follows the estrangement of the intellectuals is the adjective "curious" appropriately applied. There were voices of dissent, of course, and had been: the ebb of the tide was setting in. Frank Norris, Jack London (who began as a believer), Lincoln Steffens, Theodore Dreiser—the chorus of voices of the new wave that would challenge Fiske's too easy optimism was already swelling and about to break. Those men who created the image of John Fiske were the old guard, and perhaps they knew it; but at that moment they still had force and power.

To sustain an analogy too long is awkward and dangerous,

but the image of the tide is apt; it serves to remind us that in the rise and fall of ideologies and reputations, there is usually no abrupt change, and there is a retention of the same elements, however different they may appear in ebb and flow. The ideas which Fiske propounded were not discarded and their influence —if not his own—can still be heard and felt. In adjusting our portrait of Fiske, it is not the ideas themselves that we must judge, for their effect is clearly traceable and significant; rather, it is the extent to which Fiske was instrumental in propagating and disseminating ideas throughout the land. The modern picture, which sees Fiske as a great popularizer, has its roots directly in the eulogies by his contemporaries. The emphasis has shifted, the tone is different, and the prophecy of greatness as a thinker strongly rejected; but the keynote remains: here is a man who played effectively the role of spreading the word—a word important in its own day and important in American intellectual history, if only as a thesis to react against.

II *The Philosopher in Retrospect*

The impact of Darwinism on Western thought and culture is immeasurable. In literature alone, this influence swept in a whole new school and altered beyond redemption the evaluation of Romantics and Realists alike. In America, for example, re-evaluations had to be made (and later corrected) of Longfellow and Howells, of Whitman and Mark Twain. But, from the first, the effects of Darwinism moved in two directions: the attempt to reconcile the new science with the old theology and the insistence that no reconciliation was possible. It all swung on whether one could reaffirm the position of man as little lower than the angels or relocate him as little higher than the apes, or whether evolution could be proved a new version of the divine plan or the operation of blind forces. Not that the task was this simple, of course, for there was also the question of whether the universe was a machine with man as a cog or whether he could control his destiny; and many, John Fiske among them, held diverse views on various aspects of the questions. The over-all influence of Fiske as a philosopher and its ultimate importance depend almost entirely on the acceptance of the philosophy of Spencer and of the concept that philosophy moves along progressive or positive lines. And at least until recently that philosophy, after its brief period in the limelight, is the one that has been rejected for its optimism and its doctrine of laissez faire.

"Spencer's adaptation of Darwinism was an attempt to prove that the emergence of man's consciousness, historical and political institutions, and even his ethical values were part of the total evolutionary process. Since this process was always in the direction of higher, more complex and more stable forms of life, human society would, in the inevitable course of things, become wholly stable and orderly, and thus the long sought-for Utopia would be realized... all that man had to do was let the cosmic process sweep on to its triumphant end and not worry about minor adjustments along the way.... The resulting social conditions, unfortunately, proved to be far from Utopian."[5]

Fiske would in all likelihood have objected to the word "Utopia" (as Spencer may also have done), since utopia was a man-made Eden, and the word itself was directly opposite to the idea of noninterference with God's plan. He had so firmly fixed in mind both the concept of eternity and of cosmic process that ultimate perfection was too remote to consider. Although he maintained belief in inevitable perfectibility, he was so taken with evolution as process that despite talk of goals, he never paid any real attention to conclusions or to a state of balance. His comments on this phase of the process almost invariably lapse into theological quotations usually taken directly from the Bible.

A rather remarkable little essay of 1873 shows how completely Fiske accepted the basic lines of the description of Spencerian philosophy cited above and yet how wide open his eyes were to the actual situation in his own lifetime. The essay, "Athenian and American Life," begins with a sketch of Greek life. Turning from Athens to America, Fiske presents a scene which echoes all of the unpleasant things said about the United States by Dickens and Arnold. Somewhat later, in a review of Jackson's democracy, he was to cite both Dickens' *Martin Chuzzlewit* and Mrs. Trollope's *Domestic Manners of the Americans* as honest pictures of an earlier America. But in 1873 Fiske did not find things so greatly changed. Ironically, were the date erased from this essay, one could pass off portions of it as written in the 1970's. The modern term "rat-race" sums it all up—America is without culture and consists of hurry, hurry, hurry. "The test of complete social life is the opportunity which it affords for complete individual life. Tried by this test, our contemporary civilization will appear seriously defective,— excellent only as a preparation for something better."

This last clause is the key. Speaking of incessant turmoil, the rage for the accumulation of wealth, and the jostling and trampling on one another, Fiske is sure that these characteristics represent a transitional phase of development. He sees the advance of the machine, the slow decline of unskilled labor, the end of frontier life. But, from all of this change, he sees an age when all will attain a normal standard of comfortable living and when the appetite for great wealth will disappear. Thus, with more leisure, "it may be that there will ultimately exist, over the civilized world, conditions as favorable to the complete fruition of life as those which formerly existed within the narrow circuit of Attica; save that part once played by enslaved human brain and muscle will finally be played by the enslaved forces of insentient nature. Society will at last bear the test of providing for the complete development of its individual members."[6] The whole passage contains a striking contrast between the concrete picture of life as it was going on around him, incisively sketched, and the vague and lofty generalities about future perfection.

Among American Spencerians, the career of William Graham Sumner bears comparison with that of Fiske. In spite of many parallels in background and approach, the two men appear not to have been in any way interested in working together to promote the work of Spencer. Although both were speakers at the farewell dinner which concluded the philosopher's visit to America, I can find no other reference to Sumner in Fiske's letters. And this lack is in striking contrast to the friendly interchange between Fiske and Youmans. From general histories of Social Darwinism which summarize the ideas of leading figures, it is often possible to see Fiske's thinking in quotations from Sumner, except that the latter appears to place a stronger emphasis on the area of economics—and moved away from the questions and language of religion while Fiske moved toward them.

One concrete way of illustrating the effect of the new science is to examine a few illustrations of the result in fiction. A whole study can be made of the sociological or psychological aspects alone by using only the works of George Eliot or Henry James as a focal point. After them, the entire theory of character was different; they mark a turning point in the history of the novel in English. Both were acquaintances of Fiske, and he admired Eliot tremendously as a writer, yet it seems never to have occurred to him to examine them as artists affected by the new psychology. Henry James he never mentioned in any capacity other than social, and he extolled Eliot for the same virtues of morality, character drawing, and narrative ability that won praise for Dickens or Scott. But the novel had changed—more through the same forces in thought that had provided background for Darwin than through Darwin or Spencer directly.

Richard Eastman, presenting the question from a modern and relatively sophisticated point of view, sketches in the responses of a raw soldier in battle, balancing the combative instinct against the instinct for self-preservation, and he notes that all soldiers would not react alike. He might have added that the same individual would respond differently at different times—as Stephen Crane's Henry Fleming so ably demonstrates in *The Red Badge of Courage*. And here Eastman is focused on a specific situation and makes no judgment about whether there is any moral involved, whether the fittest is or is not the best, or the question of whether the response to environment is progressive or merely blind force. In a passage more directly concerned with the history of fiction, Eastman makes it clear that the Naturalists moved in a direction opposite to that of Fiske and Spencer:

Darwin's own stark record of the struggle of animals prompted a zoological rawness in much naturalistic fiction. Man was often described as an animal, with attention to his bone structure, musculature, and feral capacities for reproduction and self-preservation. Climaxes often turned on such appetites as hunger and lust, such basic glandular reactions as fear and rage. Plot often centered on elemental survival situations. . . . Clearly the scientific curiosity of naturalism did not prohibit the excitements of melodrama.[7]

In American literature, an excellent example is the work of Jack London, much of which may be characterized by the above passage. But more subtle than *The Call of the Wild* or *The Sea-Wolf* was *Martin Eden*. And the latter is particularly appropriate to our consideration because Martin, on his way up, was guided by his reading of Fiske and Spencer. Of London himself it was said that from Spencer and his popularizers he accepted the thesis that man evolved from the lower forms of life, differing from them only in degree rather than in kind, and he followed the doctrines of the "synthetic" philosophy through a positive faith in progress and a benevolent anarchy of Anglo-American supremacy that would allow both social and individual harmony and completeness. Obviously at least one of the younger writers was reading Fiske, if Fiske did not read any of them.

The same comment might be made of Martin, London's alter ego. The latter emerged into the kind of society that in many ways paralleled the audiences of John Fiske, and Martin ultimately found it sterile, fear-ridden, and middle-class. The reality would not square with the dream, and in the end Martin committed suicide—as did London himself. More than any other novel *Martin Eden* is apropos because it portrays a young man of the people who pins his faith on the Fiske doctrine and earns from it a bitter and empty disillusionment. Not that this condemns the philosophy: it is but a single example and a fictional one at that, though semiautobiographical. But it is not atypical, and it does suggest that whatever truths Spencer may have grasped, he did not offer the Truth for life itself.

But perhaps Fiske's reading of Spencer, more than the philosophy itself, set him apart from the younger literary artists. Most of them, like Dreiser, saw the opposite side of the coin. Dreiser read Spencer's *First Principles* in his youth and shared with Fiske only the fact that he never recovered. The book blew him to bits and "all that he deemed essential—man's place in nature, his importance in the universe . . . man's very identity save as an infinitesimal speck of energy" dissolved.[8] London's Wolf Larsen saw no moral value in the new science, nothing of right and wrong: "Good and evil? Those were the toys of clerics, by which they made money. Morality and immorality? He never considered them. But strength and weakness—oh yes, if you had strength you could protect yourself always and be something. If you were weak—pass quickly to the rear and out of range of the guns."[9]

The interpretations prevalent in fiction were paralleled in other fields, and this very reading of Darwin Fiske had devoted his energies to disproving. Yet it stemmed, at least in part, from the same sources as his own philosophy; and at least for a time it was the view which captured American thought. While Fiske himself never came into direct conflict with these literary Naturalists, there were voices of protest which at least from a moral or ethical angle were closer to Fiske. And among later historians, Henry Steele Commager finds the whole movement doomed by its own lack of logic. For, he says, "revolt is an act of will—even of free will—and those writers who engage in it confess their inconsistency. They confess faith in their appeal for a hearing, and recognition of a moral order by the establishment of standards, however esoteric."[10] Fiske would not have argued in these terms nor, of course, does this imply that Commager would support Fiske; nevertheless, they are in basic agreement that the negative approach denies truth and therefore that such a thing as truth exists or it could not be denied. There may be here indications that the philosophy of Fiske needs to be reassessed—that it is less ephemeral than has for a time appeared to be the case.

While Fiske proclaimed himself to be a disciple of Spencer and while that aspect of his philosophy has received most attention, there were other influences at work. When he was a boy wrestling with religious problems, the Reverend Dudley had introduced him to both Theodore Parker and Emerson. For a long time this reading seemed to have been in good part forgotten, but it only lay buried; and, as he turned more and more toward religion, much of it returned to the surface. In Fiske's rejection of special creation, in his separation of the Jesus of history from the Christ of dogma, and in his method of depicting God—except for a more scientific slant of language—Fiske echoes strongly the ideas expressed by Parker in "A Discourse Pertaining to Matters of Religion." For instance, such a comment as "there is a natural supply for spiritual as well as corporeal wants; . . . a connection between God and the soul, as between light and the eye, sound and the ear, food and the palate, truth and the intellect, beauty and the imagination. . . ."[11] comes from

Parker, but it might as well be from one of John Fiske's "sermons." So, too, Parker's assessment of Emerson strikes upon qualities that Fiske admired; "the Idea of America, which lies at the bottom of our original institutions, appears in him with great prominence. We mean the idea of personal freedom, of the dignity and value of human nature, the superiority of a man to the accidents of a man."[12] That Fiske had not forgotten Parker is evidenced by his visit to the latter's grave in Florence and by his wonder that Parker had chosen this place as a refuge from consumption.

The personal visit to Emerson when John was at the beginning of his college career made a profound impression, and he never lost his regard for the elder philosopher. It is often said, of course, that Emerson was many things to many men, and perhaps the clearest statement of what Fiske found valuable in his ideas is recorded in Fiske's conversation with John Spencer Clark about Emerson. Naturally enough, Fiske was most interested in the awareness which Emerson showed in what John called nascent evolutionary theories. He cited phrases such as "the continuous adjustment of internal relations to external relations," and he found an evolutionary quality in Emerson's well-known version of the great chain of being: "a subtle chain of countless rings. . . ." Naturally, Fiske was also impressed by Emerson's penetrating observation of the physical and chemical sciences of his own time; but more important was Emerson's concept of God.

Clark suggested that Emerson had met resistance because his idea of God "was much too impersonal, much too abstract to satisfy the demand of the time for a personal God, for a Divine Creator distinctly knowable through human experience."[13] Agreeing thoroughly, Fiske read from Cabot's *Memoir* a passage taken from Emerson's diary of 1838:

I say that I cannot find, when I explore my own consciousness, any truth in saying that God is a person, but the reverse. I feel that there is some profanation in saying he is personal. To represent him as an individual is to shut him out of my consciousness. He is then but a great man, such as the crowd worship. The natural motions of the soul are so much better than the voluntary ones that you will never do yourself justice in a dispute. . . . I deny personality to God, because it is too little, not too much—Life, personal life, is faint and cold to the energy of God.[14]

And Fiske contended that this was precisely the explanation of Spencer's Unknowable and of his own Idea of God.

Possibly nothing shows so sharply the American quality of Fiske's outlook than this mixture of Transcendentalism and Spencerian science. That there was warrant for it is suggested by Spencer's own deep interest in Emerson, but it took an American mind to amalgamate the two. In closing, Clark defines Fiske's achievement in this area of philosophy as "a happy blending of the poetic philosophico-religious insights of Emerson with the profound scientific truths established by Spencer and Darwin."[15] Fiske himself probably came even closer to defining his own appeal, as well as that of Spencer, when he wrote: "Spencer's generalizations give us a complete and scientific statement of a truth which in more or less vague and imperfect shape permeates the intellectual atmosphere of our time."[16]

Fiske, not an esthetician, offers no comprehensive theory of esthetics; but his deep interest in the arts and his insistence on the literary nature of his own career make it valuable to summarize some of his ideas about this area of human ability. Underlying his preferences among writers, artists, and musicians, as well as his goals in his own writing, were certain principles for judging. Most concrete among these was the definition of a poet as set forth in his evaluation of Milton: "the true poet is far more than a builder of rhymes; he is the man who sees the deepest truths that concern humanity, and knows how to proclaim them with power and authority such as no other kind of man save the poet can wield."[17] In another connection, the term "poet," is broadened to include the novelist and the orator; in oratory, Daniel Webster most nearly meets the ideal—at least in modern history. Fiske singles out his speeches for "religious devotion to the union" and, more directly focusing on their literary values, for "the fine sense of proportion and fitness, the massive weight of argument due to transparent clearness and matchless symmetry of statement, and along with the rest a truly Attic simplicity of diction." These qualities Fiske himself cultivated, and the rest of his encomium sounds like praise later given to Fiske by his admirers: "Mr. Webster never indulged in mere rhetorical flights; his sentences, simple in structure and weighted with meaning, went straight to the mark; and his arguments were so skillfully framed that, while his most learned and critical hearers were impressed with a sense of their conclusiveness, no man of ordinary intelligence could fail to understand them."[18] And it was for these qualities that "the historian must assign to them a high place among the literary influences that aroused in the American people a sentiment of union strong enough to endure the shock of war."[19] This classification of the orator as a literary man reminds us both of the great tradition of oratory and of the importance of this role in Fiske's own life and work.

On the more abstract level, Fiske interested himself most specifically in the psychology of art or in the nature of the artistic mind and soul. In *Cosmic Philosophy* he makes two notable points: one on the individual quality of human perceptions and the other on the importance of developing natural abilities through training. Noting that response differs in accordance with environing relationships, individual sagacity, and the extent of experience, Fiske uses among his illustrations the reading of the sky by a practiced mariner and an unskilled passenger. And "A cartoon by Raphael or a symphony of Beethoven will excite different emotions in an artist and a person of feeble impressibility."[20] By implication, Fiske appears to say that the untaught genius has developed only a portion of his powers, great as it may be. "In the fine arts . . . the superiority imparted by systematic instruction is incontestable. Doubtless it is by long-continued practice that men learn to paint pictures, to mould statues, and to compose oratorios or symphonies. But it is none the less probable that Mozart and Beethoven would have accomplished comparatively little without the profound study of harmony; and in painting and sculpture the 'originality of untaught geniuses' is, not unjustly, made a subject for sarcasm."[21]

An essay on Lessing's "Nathan the Wise" has more of a Romantic twist. In it, men are divided into two types of genius: the poetical and the philosophical, or the artistic and the critical. And, at this point, there is no question that Fiske finds the former superior, the genius which sees things in all their natural complexity as contrasted with the genius which pulls things to pieces analytically. "The former sees a tree in all its glory, where the latter sees an exogen with a pair of cotyledons. The former sees wholes where the latter sees aggregates." Or, when the critical genius sets out to write a poem or paint a picture, he begins with prearranged theory or chooses the mood; he does not truly create but constructs and combines. The artistic genius "sees the picture or hears the symphony with the eyes and ears of imagination, and paints and plays merely what he has seen or heard." The coin has been flipped to the reverse side—the focus is now not on the formal training but on the innate difference of perception.

The literary example is Dante, with his wonderfully vivid pictures of Hell. "So Michael Angelo, a kindred genius, did not keep cutting and chipping away, thinking how Moses ought to look, and what sort of nose he ought to have, and in what position his head might rest on his shoulders. But he looked at the rectangular block of Carrara marble, and beholding Moses grand and lifelike within it, knocked away the environing stone, that others might also see the mighty figure." Innate perception, he maintains, is demonstrated by modern psychology. "It is therefore apt to be a barren criticism which studies the works of creative geniuses in order to ascertain what theory lies beneath them. How many systems of philosophy, how many subtle speculations, have we not seen fathered upon Dante, Cervantes, Shakespeare, and Goethe! Yet their works are, in a certain sense, greater than any systems. They partake of the infinite complexity and variety of nature, and no more than nature itself can they be narrowed down to the limits of a precise formula."[22] Undoubtedly Fiske regarded himself as predominantly of the philosophical or critical cast, but he pointed out that all persons possessed both kinds of imagination to some extent. It is, therefore, no wonder that he made no attempt to set down any organized esthetic or creative theory and that he always hoped in writing his history to "put some poetry" into the narrative.

Turning our attention to the field of formal philosophy, we find one aspect of John Fiske's *Outlines of Cosmic Philosophy* that strikes a remarkably modern note. Very recently, Allen Tate made the following observation:

Of the philosophers I likewise speak with neither information nor knowledge. Like Mr. Santayana, I might somewhat presumptuously describe myself as "an ignorant man, almost a poet." But one gets strongly the impression that the classical metaphysical question— What is the nature of Being?—is semantically meaningless in our age, a mere historicism reserved for the frivolous occasions of the lecture-room philosophy. Our going philosophy is reported to me as a curious, apostolic activity known as the "philosophy of science," an attempt to devise a language for all of the sciences which through it would arrive at "unity." This is a laudable program, unity usually being better than disunity, unless the things joined together dislike each other, or, again, unless the union takes place at a level of abstraction at which certain things become excluded, such as human nature. . . .[23]

John Fiske would have protested at the final objection implied, for he, too, recognized the importance of human nature. But, as far back as his *Outlines of Cosmic Philosophy*, this role is the one that he demanded philosophy play. The question about the nature of being belonged strictly in the realm of metaphysics, and that realm should be left to religion. Philosophy's greatest task was to prove itself the greatest of the sciences, the synthesizer; and, almost in the same words as Tate, Fiske pointed out that philosophy properly handled would find the language for all of the sciences and thus demonstrate their unity.

While this discussion might seem to prove that modern philosophy has come around to Fiske, the case is not quite that simple. I am assured by philosophers that Tate cites a movement by the Vienna circle in the 1930's, a movement which has quite gone out of favor. But, for that matter, formal philosophers never did accept Herbert Spencer; and today they regard him as an ill-informed amateur. Logically, this attitude would imply that John Fiske has not been accepted into the guild. We could add that the situation becomes additionally complicated by the fact that, in later books, Fiske himself turned his attention quite thoroughly to religious questions. However he may have defined them, or rationalized that they were both philosophical and scientific, such works as *The Destiny of Man* and *Through Nature to God* contain large portions which are both metaphysical and religious in essence—argue as the author will that his view remains scientific and that this duality is precisely what the basic concept of cosmic or synthetic permits.

What we do demonstrate is that ideas which John Fiske propounded continued to be heard within the boundaries if not in the capitals of formal philosophy. As late as the 1950's, Allen Tate was exposed to these ideas, whether from philosophers directly or through a rather long grapevine does not particularly affect the argument. There may indeed be a major problem in exactly how Fiske should be classified, what his proper niche is to be; but that he played a part in the history of ideas is inescapable. The history of philosophy may well be written without more than a footnote on Spencer and silence on Fiske, but the history of nineteenth-century thought in England and America cannot honestly pass by either of them.

III   *The Historian in Perspective*

When John Fiske turned to the study of American history, it was largely because of Mrs. Hemenway's appeal for lectures at Old South Church. Yet Fiske found an area which he felt had been neglected. The reaction of the public to the American past was demonstrated by the fact that Parkman's great study of Pontiac lay untouched on the publisher's shelves for years. It was reflected in the question asked of Parkman: "Why don't you take some European subject,—something that people will be interested in? . . . Nobody cares to read about what happened out here in the woods a hundred years ago."[24] Proposing to give some lectures about "America's Place in History" in a small New England town, Fiske ran into the same indifference. Asking if he would find a good audience, he was told, "The subject is one which would interest very few people."[25] In general, it was assumed that America had no past, no history.

Delivering his anniversary address in Middletown in 1900, Fiske cites the idea often expressed by Hawthorne and James that there is nothing of romance about the subject; but John Fiske completely rejects this belief. Not only, as he said earlier in writing of Parkman, did America have as much fascination as Scott found in his border country; but, in effect, the history of America was already as long as that of Rome "from the beginning of the Punic Wars to the reign of Augustus and twice as long as that of Athens."[26] Furthermore, Fiske felt that it was as important as any period in all Western history because of the American development of representative government—if nothing else. Later historians support the feeling that nineteenth-century America was not particularly concerned with her own history—ironically, in part, because of the same optimistic attitude of looking forward toward the future rather than back to the past which Fiske's own philosophizing promoted. If he had done nothing else, his work in building that interest was, indeed, a great contribution to American culture.

More than once Fiske paused to define the way in which history should be written. Often, his theories of evolution and his cosmic views gave a list to starboard; often, the actual writing was somewhat remote from the definitions. But, when directly commenting on what he called the "new history," he ever maintained that careful scholarship and a study of primary sources were of the utmost importance. "Or we must fall back upon the remark, half humorous, half cynical, once made by Sainte-Beuve, that History is, in large part, a set of fables that men have agreed to believe in."[27]

Sainte-Beuve, says Fiske, should have used the past tense because historians are no longer willing merely to copy their predecessors; they insist on original sources of information to correct the fables: "the statutes, diplomatic correspondence, the reports and general orders of commanding officers, the records of debates in councils and parliaments, ships' log-books, political pamphlets, printed sermons, contemporary memoirs, private diaries and letters, newspapers, broadsides and placards, even perhaps to worm-eaten account books and files of receipts." Elsewhere, Fiske adds the very great value of town records. The method one uses in analyzing these various records is to attempt to uncover true cause and effect; "real knowledge is attained only when the events of a period are studied in their causal relations to one another amid all their concrete complexity."[28] And the proper purpose is that we may first have an accurate interpretation of history in order that correct lessons may be drawn from it. Such was the foundation upon which Fiske built his historical structure.

In order to make some judgment about the significance of Fiske as a historian, it is wise to draw back that we may see the woods for the trees. Behind him stood the works of Sparks and Bancroft; immediately behind him the great Romantic historians: Prescott, Motley, and Parkman, only one of whom dealt directly with American history. Beside him stood Henry Adams, Moses Coit Tyler, and, in England, John Green and Edward Freeman. And beyond him were to come F. J. Turner, Vernon Parrington, and Charles Beard. We do not suggest, however, that the historians listed are of equal stature, nor that they are the only significant historians America has produced; instead, they serve as representatives of the course of American historiography, and each in his way touched upon the work of Fiske. In a sense, we can almost measure the importance of each, or his modern reputation, by the number of pages assigned to him in present-day histories of the growth and development of American thought. If this quantitative measure has any validity, John Fiske is at least among those who cannot be overlooked.

Fiske refers often to Bancroft when naming historians of the day, and at one point he prefaces his name with the phrase "eminent historian"; but he seems to have been little influenced by the work of the older writer. Reading the theories expressed in Bancroft's "On the Progress of Civilization," one is a little surprised that he did not carry more weight with Fiske as there are a number of notable parallels. Yet Bancroft carried his belief in progress to the point of active participation in politics and to an outspoken belief in reform and the masses. Neither of these approaches would have been acceptable to Fiske. As we have seen, he deplored reform as interference with the natural evolutionary process; and, in spite of his faith in mankind and in representative government, Fiske really leaned toward the ideas of Alexander Hamilton and Hugh Henry Brackenridge regarding the weaknesses of the electorate that formulated majority rule. Progress, to Fiske, came from God through human leaders who were superior to the rest—never through the voice of the mass of the people.

Fiske had read fairly extensively both Motley and Prescott, and he clearly preferred the former. Prescott, it would seem, was a bit too elegant for John Fiske. Motley treats tyranny with more disrespect, frankly calling Philip II a rake, a bigot, a burglar, and an assassin, instead of speaking of his "arbitrary and somewhat unscrupulous policy."[29] Amusingly, in reviewing Motley's work on Spain and the Netherlands, Fiske carried plain talk about Philip a step further. Comparing Philip to his father, Charles—though both were tyrants—was like comparing a boor with a gentleman: "Both were terrible gluttons, a fact which puritanic criticism might set down as equally to the discredit of each of them. But even in intemperance there are degrees of refinement, and the impartial critic of life and manners will no doubt say that if one must get drunk, let it be on *Château Margaux* rather than on commissary whiskey. Pickled partridges, plump capons, syrups of fruits, delicate pastry, and rare fish went to make up the diet of Charles in his last days at Yeste. But the beastly Philip would make himself sick with a surfeit of underdone pork."[30]

This distinction Fiske could appreciate, but Prescott's refinements of language were sheer euphemism; for, as Fiske asserted, "Motley is a historian of the people, Prescott of Kings and Nobles; so that, although Prescott is a rather better writer, I consider Motley much more of a historian. Motley's style is a little jerkey and mannerish, but it has a vitality."[31] This statement is as much a revelation of John Fiske's own interests perhaps as it is a way of relating him to his great predecessors. Fiske, conscious of style and language level, loves to accent his straightforward way of speaking. And Motley's subject, dealing with the Dutch people—burgher and Protestant as they were—would be more appealing. Prescott did not at all agree with Fiske's evolutionary analysis of the aboriginal Americans or of the Aztec or Inca civilizations. Yet these lines of comparison do relate him to the earlier men in that there is a continued Romanticism in Fiske which concerns itself with style and which is underscored by Fiske's constantly thinking of himself as engaged in a "literary" career. For all of his scientific history, he would have preferred the title of "man of letters"; like his predecessors, he was still a man who believed that history should be written as a narrative with a theme.

Were not Parkman a colleague and personal friend of Fiske, he might be classified with his compatriots in this analysis. Closer to him, Fiske was more strongly influenced—to the point of borrowing rather heavily, at least in the first draft of his *New France and New England*. At times the interchange between the two men looks like the record of a meeting of a mutual admiration society. Of Parkman, Fiske writes: "These pages are alive with political philosophy, and teem with object lessons of extraordinary value. It would be hard to point to any book where History more fully discharges her high function of gathering friendly lessons of caution from the errors of the past." And he continues: "Great in his natural powers and great in the use he has made of them, Francis Parkman was no less great in his occasion and his theme. Of all American historians he is the most deeply and peculiarly American yet at the same time he is the broadest and most cosmopolitan."[32] Earlier Parkman had been consulted about Fiske's turning to history and had written: "As to the Short History of the American people, I strongly advise you to go into it. If you are able to give it the necessary time and attention, I am sure they will be well invested in all senses. I believe you could do the work better than anybody else."[33]

Parkman's death brought forth a memorial two-part essay by Justin Winsor and John Fiske, and the points of emphasis in the two portions of the essay reveal much about Fiske's own histories—regardless of theories or thesis. Winsor, who reviews Parkman's background and concerns himself with scholarship and history per se, emphasizes the distinction between the old and the new historians: the older ones "had subjected historical documents, especially of the contributions of actors in the scene, to the revisions of the pedagogue. It was a fashion never stronger anywhere than in New England, where the characteristics of ancestors have always been viewed tenderly." Parkman, representing the new view, felt that such a practice violated the integrity of history; the actual record was the true one. "In mending the style and orthography, or even the grammar," he said, "one may rob a passage of its characteristic expression, till it ceases to mark the individuality of the man, or the nature of his antecedents and surroundings."[34] Winsor also focuses on the question of pure history with his comment that Parkman avoided philosophical sentiment, letting the course of events carry its own philosophy. It should be added that by "philosophical sentiment" Winsor meant an explicit summary of the lesson to be learned from the historical events under consideration; he did not mean to imply that there was no philosophy underlying Parkman's work.

For Winsor, Parkman's great achievement was in blending art and history: "It was his faithfulness to an artistic ideal, no less than a steady adherence to his plan, that Parkman stood for."[35] Contrasting the modern spirit with the old, Winsor adds that much "of what we read for history is simply the accretion, inherited from many generations of narrators, of opinions, of prejudices, and sentiments. . . . It requires some courage to strip the mummied facts of these cerements of sympathies." Parkman had courage, for example, in dealing with the Acadians and in daring "to tell the world that the figments which make a poem [Longfellow's *Evangeline*] are not the truths that underlie the story."[36]

There are many places where we can find these points paralleled in Fiske's own writing. He had even demonstrated that Longfellow was a great myth-builder and poet, but not always a historian though he chose not *Evangeline* but *Hiawatha* as his example. However, in this essay, Fiske's analysis sounds more like the evaluation of a historical novelist than of a historian; for he underlines the romantic possibilities of American history. "The Alleghanies as well as the Apennines have looked down on great causes lost and won, and the Mohawk Valley is classic ground no less than the banks of the Rhine."[37] He speaks of Parkman's realistic pictures and detailed narrative, and he compares his subject with Sir Walter Scott and James Fenimore Cooper rather than with other historians. It is true that he sees this realism as reflecting the scientific concern with truth, and it is also true that he does contrast Prescott and Parkman with respect to this point of fact versus myth.

Still, Fiske's comment is in terms of narrative: Parkman's Indians are true to life, and "in his pages Pontiac is a man of warm flesh and blood," but in Prescott "one feels oneself in the world of Arabian Nights . . . his Montezuma is a personality like none that ever existed beneath the moon." Although Fiske pays careful tribute to Parkman's scholarship, his whole essay echoes with attention to narrative, drama, and color. In fact, the key to his entire approach is his definition of the historian: "Into the making of a historian there should enter something of a philosopher, something of the naturalist, something of the poet."[38] We might well conclude with the observation that Winsor set forth a concept of history with which Fiske theoretically was in full accord, while Fiske himself—definitions and statements of purpose to the contrary—admired in Parkman the very characteristics which are notable in his own histories. Fiske, in describing what he liked and admired in a dear friend and revered master, came closer to describing his own work than he ever did when intentionally setting forth his aims and methods.

Parkman, too, was a help on the Indian question. From the earliest times there had been debate about the character of the red man, and by the eighteenth century it had focused on the views of Rousseau about the noble savage. In American literature, James Fenimore Cooper became the whipping boy of those who leaned more toward the concept that a good Indian is a dead one. Among the many who found Uncas too good to be true was Francis Parkman, who wrote: "jointly with Thomas Campbell, Cooper is responsible for the fathering of those aboriginal heroes, lovers, and sages, who have long formed a petty nuisance in our literature."[39]

Parkman's argument was that this romanticizing was untrue to history; and, needless to say, Fiske agreed with Parkman. Rousseau's concept was too far out of line with the evolutionist idea that Indians were savages and therefore automatically inferior to civilized white men; and upon the idea of savagery Fiske based his entire interpretation. And, indeed, leaving all theories out of the picture, it becomes next to impossible to determine which side came closer to the historical truth. There are those who condemn Fiske for a careless treatment of history, but among other historians in his own time—or the generation just previous—analysis was divided.

On the question of King Philip and his war, for example (and it was on this question that Fiske's critics attacked), Palfrey and Oliver presented two opposing views. Theodore Roosevelt made it clear that he accepted the evolutionary view, at least the point of regarding the red race as inferior; and he called for a cessation of sentimental nonsense about our conquest of them and of the continent. In short, during the nineteenth century just about every historian and man of letters who dealt with the American scene joined the debate. And, in examining the various opinions, there is little point in choosing sides; to retain our own historical perspective, we can but note the position that Fiske took among the rest.

Parallels between John Fiske and Henry Adams are intriguing, if not literally striking. Of not dissimilar New England background, both were graduates of Harvard—Adams, in 1858; Fiske, in 1863; each had been reserved but sufficiently active to gain a part in commencement ceremonies (Adams, class orator; Fiske, class poet); both had taught at Harvard (Fiske almost succeeding Adams in the history department); both came to history the long way around; and both thoroughly absorbed the new science. Though they are divergent in many or all major aspects of their thinking and writing, there is enough comparison to make for a very interesting and very solid least common denominator. And there is perhaps nothing which tells us more of the nature of Fiske as a historian—if not his quality—than placing side by side his history of the American people with that of Adams.

By a curious paradox, such a study shows Fiske to be much more a man of his times, while Adams is generally far more aware of the world around him. Born, as Adams said, out of his time, he had a keener perspective than the man who belonged to the age. A single notable illustration is Adams' awareness of the coming importance of Russia and the United States; in looking to the future, Fiske dreamed rather than saw England and the United States. But both men saw early the dangers that pointed toward World War I. In all justice, we must acknowledge that Adams' comment on Russia comes from *The Education of Henry Adams*, which dealt with contemporary matters, and that Fiske in his history never progressed beyond the inauguration of George Washington.

And in the story of colonial America both saw the vital part played by transportation and communication—the debt owed by America to the steamboat and the railroad. On the other hand, each colored his history with his own particular vision; and the difference is that Adams saw cataclysm where Fiske saw Manifest Destiny. Ultimately, Adams' longer view has proved him the better historian. But he, too, had his rise and fall; and finally we must be reminded of John Fiske's vision when we see the title of a later great historical work, *The History of the English-Speaking Peoples,* by Sir Winston Churchill.

Fiske's progressive evolutionary view, minus the focus on Anglo-America, echoes through phrases like "The Great Society" and "The New Frontier" (though in our more sophisticated fashion we have come to believe that evolution can be progressive but that it is our right and duty to prod it into a forward march). John F. Kennedy's phrase reminds us how completely the historical thinking of our own generation is linked to the ideas of Frederick Jackson Turner, and Turner shares with Fiske a strong belief in the theories of evolution. In a sense, Turner was a successor to Parkman; and the strong difference in style and tone between the two can also be seen in the differences between Turner and Fiske. Beyond these questions of style and tone, there was also a vast difference in approach to evolution; for as Commager comments, "[Turner's] was not the kind of evolution John Fiske was teaching. For where Fiske emphasized inheritance, Turner emphasized environment; where Fiske liked to find the genesis of the New England town in the *folkgemot* of primitive Germany, or the liberty of the Magna Carta, or of federalism in the leagues of the Greek city-states, Turner insisted that the American environment accounted sufficiently for these and other American institutions."[40]

Commager then observes that the environmental concept appealed to a people who felt that they had created more than they had inherited, and again we see a shift of modern thinking away from John Fiske: men play an active part, a creative role in their use of environment; evolution is not a matter of waiting for the cosmos to move in its ponderous way its wonders to perform. And, while men might not care to believe that the end of the frontier would make problems, those of Fiske's day became less interested in being told that the end of the frontier would be one factor in bringing about a more stable society—there was nothing exciting about stability. As a matter of fact, John Fiske appears to have been wrong, or the world too impatient; his prophecy has not yet been fulfilled.

For all his New England outlook, John Fiske hated any provincialism, and his own personal experiences in western states gave him a broader view than generally appears. Dealing with specific men and events on a concrete level, he made a strong point of correcting the idea that the West could be passed over lightly. Eastern writers, "while freely admitting the vastness and strength of the Western country, and the picturesqueness of its annals, have utterly failed to comprehend the importance of its share in the political development of the American nation."[41] It was, Fiske felt, the Scotch-Irish of the western states with their loyalty to union greater than to individual state governments which held the nation together during the crisis of the Civil War. The movement west to the Pacific was essential to his concept of Manifest Destiny; it could not have been accomplished by a people tied to the eastern seaboard with their eyes always toward Europe. This breadth of view does not change the basic argument: he still maintained that the cause for this effect was the inherited tradition of political views and institutions. Nevertheless, we should note that, on a concrete level, Fiske was well aware that American history was not bounded on the west by the Hudson River. The cosmic view had its effect on focus, but it did lift his eyes to the Columbia River and beyond.

Between Fiske and Turner there was, then, a gap. With the advent of new generations, the gap became a chasm. Charles Beard came to the conclusion that the philosophy of history was that no philosophy could be formulated—and where does that leave a man like Fiske whose whole argument is that history serves as a noble illustration of the truth of a given philosophy? Furthermore, Beard's emphasis, as no doubt the times demanded, was on an economic view—and that John Fiske had made subsidiary. For, when the economic situation began to prove that the laissez faire concept was doing what it had promised, the philosophy of both Fiske and Spencer lost its strength with the American people. Between Fiske and Parrington, the disparity was even greater as can most clearly be seen in the younger man's conclusions.

Having devoted several pages to a thumbnail biography of Fiske—one full of sharp perceptions—Parrington ends by saying: "Not a great historian, Fiske ceased to be in his later wandering years a great intellectual influence. The rare promise of his young manhood he never fulfilled, but like his generation suffered his energies to be dissipated . . . to a later generation it is difficult to make out his great stature. Nevertheless as a pur-

veyor of Victorian science to the American people he did a useful and important work."[42]

Parrington too has his bias, but in many ways this is not an
unjust conclusion. Though varying in tone and degree, the portraits of Fiske painted by present-day students of American
cultural and intellectual history stress essentially the same points.
We are forced to grant that either they simply borrow from one
another or that their common judgment reflects something of
the truth. Parrington is supported by Richard Hofstadter, Commager, Van Wyck Brooks, and even Fiske's most recent biographer, Milton Berman.[43] Repeatedly, we are told that John
Fiske, despite his bulk, was not a giant in the earth. Yet, in
each of these studies, pages are devoted to his career or chapters are focused around his work: nowhere have I found him
relegated to a footnote. The question remains: what kind of
man is this historian who can insist upon a fair share of space
in evaluation of American thought—and still be summarized as
not a great man?

IV A Final View

The reputations of famous men have their rise and fall; eras,
too, with their way of life and thought, have a way of evoking
changing responses from the ages which follow. Particularly does
a figure or an age tend to suffer with the reaction of those which
immediately follow. In part, this factor appears to be the answer
to the varying images of John Fiske; most of the criticisms we
have seen are from a period when the Victorians were out of
favor. Although contemporary scholarship is restoring the balance, John Fiske still awaits careful reassessment. He was so
thoroughly a man of his times that he was bound to suffer, as
did his neighbors Longfellow and Lowell. Overestimated by
an enthusiastic and optimistic age, they have been underesti-
mated by those eras which followed.

For, unless we wish to make everything a matter of pure
semantics, a relativistic game in which we say "it all depends
on what you mean," it is just as well to admit that John Fiske
was not a very great and learned man. A man of prodigious
memory, an omnivorous reader—and even a man of learning
wide and broad. But a man with truly cosmic vision, of deep

and discerning wisdom—that he was not. And Fiske's theory was such that the proof of its cosmic view depended entirely upon its working out as the years went by. Still, in the end, it is a relative matter: learned in comparison to whom? How many in all of the millions of men can really claim the kind of greatness herein implied? Fiske himself would not have claimed nor have dreamed of such stature—to the end, there is in his letters the slightly awed, half-unconscious note of surprise to find himself in the company he kept. To the end, despite his rejection of the great-man theory, he was a hero worshiper, looking up to the Goethes, the Dantes, the Beethovens of the world. If he tended to place Spencer in the same company, this fact does not lessen his sense that the truly great were above him and that he did not expect to walk with them. But his friends and admirers, a large and influential segment of Americans, maintained that he did so. Had they been less enthusiastic, the reaction might not have been so great—but then they would not have been American Victorians; and no more than their successors could they be expected to act out of character.

At the risk of repetition, we reemphasize how thoroughly Fiske was a man of his times. The Victorian optimism born of anxiety, the will to believe, the earnestness and enthusiasm, the Puritan morality, the devotion to home life—in all of these qualities Fiske mirrors the times in which he lived. And, in a sense, he was a spokesman for Victorian America—at least on one level of society; but that level dominated the scene. Indeed, no student of the American past can afford to ignore him, as the number of pages he receives in recent studies well attests. We cannot honestly maintain that Fiske provides a composite or synthesis, a complete portrait of the age; it was too diverse for that. Moreover, there were some currents which never touched him, and, from the beginning, there were voices of dissent.

As has already been said, the interpretation of Darwinian philosophy which saw chaotic chance rather than divine pattern was the concept which ultimately prevailed. Nevertheless, if we wish to see more clearly the frame of mind which clung to the Spencerian approach—and to see it is essential to an understanding of the American past—the best way to do so is by studying John Fiske. In a very real way, his work was a summing up:

there was a great need that at least the attempt be made to reconcile the old religion with the new science. Fiske did a remarkable and dramatic job of achieving this synthesis; and, because of this contribution, we can finally recognize, if not accept, his great stature.

Essentially, John Fiske remains a great figure for historical reasons—because of the role he played. Granting this role, it is easy to dismiss him as important only to students of American history and culture. His various works then become valuable not so much for what they are but for what they meant and what they achieved. Dividing his work into two main categories, we can still raise a demurral. There is first his career as a lecturer. To the modern scholar, here is evidence of a dissipation of powers and a squandering of abilities; but his was an age of lecturing, as Emerson, Mark Twain, Dickens, and even Henry Thoreau knew. Given an esthetic which believed that the main task of the literary man was to educate and lead—perhaps even to preach—the lecturing becomes central. It is doubtful if Fiske would have done anything of note except against the background of the lecture platform, for a large portion of his writing was derived from his lectures, and he needed the sounding board of an audience response. It is true, of course, that this lecturing was an evanescent thing: we have no way of recapturing it to judge for ourselves the creativity or force or effectiveness of these men as lecturers.

The point is simply that the lecturer was a typical and important figure in the nineteenth-century world and that we do justice neither to the times nor the man (nor to ourselves) if we pass over this phase of Fiske's career as merely a diverting force from the great writing that he might have done. Perhaps we are too much influenced by Fiske's insistence that his was a literary career.

As for the books and the essays themselves, it is necessary to make all the concessions first. The ideas are not always original, the scholarship is sometimes neither profound nor exact, and Berman is right when he suggests that philosophers tend to praise Fiske's history while historians find him a fine philosopher. But this duality is precisely the value of a man like John Fiske; he is not easily placed in a category because his whole outlook defied boundaries. We need to be reminded of relatedness and interaction of fields of knowledge. As for the positive side of the coin, in an age of specialization which yet demands breadth of knowledge, in an age which (in spite of its specialization) is still so interrelated in all of its aspects that none of us can hope to act as citizens or even as human beings without some grasp of areas other than our own, the works of John Fiske are valuable in demonstrating this principle. Furthermore, to the nonexpert, he is helpful in making him become aware of other areas. The philosophy of the *Outlines of Cosmic Philosophy* may be dated, but its analysis does give the layman a clear concept of much that is the basis of both modern philosophy and modern science. In this work, as in all of his works, such an effect is possible because of the lucidity of Fiske's style, his breadth of scope, his imagination, his rare ability to make things concrete. The histories may be theory-ridden and not to be taken as the final word; their limitations are obvious. But they are exciting reading; Fiske knew how to tell a story.

In Fiske's histories and in his letters we can recapture a sense of the vast sweep, the romance, and the excitement of the American past. In the face of the national preservation program, we do well to catch from Fiske an awareness of this vast land that was ours before we were the land's. To fight the battles of the "new frontier" we need pragmatically to reaffirm our faith in the dignity of man. For a most delightful dose of romantic optimism (mix it, if you will, with a good dash of skeptic bitters to give astringency), John Fiske can still play his role of preacher and guide to Western society.

Notes and References

Chapter One

1. John Fiske, "The Story of a New England Town," *Atlantic Monthly*, LXXXVI (December, 1900), p. 733. The article is a reprint of an address delivered October 10, 1900, at the 250th anniversary of the founding of Middletown.
2. Ethel F. Fisk, *The Letters of John Fiske* (New York, 1940), p. 10. See bibliography for comment on the dependability of this volume.
3. *Ibid.*, p. 12.
4. "Thomas Jefferson, The Conservative Reformer," *Essays Historical and Literary* (New York, 1902), I, 175.
5. *Letters*, p. 1. See also John Spencer Clark, *John Fiske, Life and Letters* (Boston and New York, 1917), I, 36. A number of Fiske letters can be cross-referenced between these two volumes.
6. The final "e" was added later upon his registration at Harvard. Evidently clerks were as capable as computers of misspelling students' names on college registrations. In any event, John looked back to his ancestors and chose to retain the "e" for the rest of his life.
7. *Letters*, p. 4.
8. *Ibid.*, p. 2.
9. Clark, I, 65.
10. *Letters*, p. 32.
11. *Ibid.*, p. 16.
12. *Ibid.*, p. 18.
13. *Ibid.*, p. 21.
14. *Ibid.*, p. 26.
15. *Ibid.*, p. 27. Also Clark, I, 87.
16. *New France and New England* (Boston and New York, 1904), p. 193.
17. *Ibid.*, p. 200.

Chapter Two

1. Clark, I, 114.
2. *Ibid.*, p. 117.
3. *Letters*, p. 32.
4. *Ibid.*, p. 33.

5. *Ibid.*

6. *Ibid.*, p. 35.

7. Clark, I, 139.

8. Manuscript Autobiographical Notes, Henry Huntington Library, cited by Milton Berman, *John Fiske* (Cambridge, 1961), p. 28.

9. Clark, I, 167.

10. *Ibid.*, p. 237.

11. *Letters*, p. 93. Where several quotations in one paragraph are from exactly the same source, I have annotated only the final quotation.

12. *Ibid.*, p. 45.

13. *Ibid.*, p. 40.

14. *Ibid.*, p. 53.

15. Catherine Drinker Bowen, *Yankee from Olympus* (Boston, 1944), p. 120. I have chosen this volume for comparison for three reasons: its excellent coverage, the fact that Holmes was at Harvard during the same period as Fiske, and the fact that the two men were social acquaintances, possibly friends.

16. *Letters*, pp. 37 and 41.

17. *Ibid.*, p. 102.

18. "Alexander Hamilton and the Federalist Party," *Essays Historical and Literary*, I, 123.

19. *Letters*, p. 52.

20. *Yankee from Olympus*, p. 135.

21. Berman, p. 46.

22. *Letters*, p. 70.

23. *Ibid.*, p. 68.

24. Berman, p. 29. From "List of Future Plans," in Harvard Class of 1863, Manuscript Class Book, p. 941.

25. *Letters*, pp. 107 and 119.

26. *Ibid.*, p. 135.

27. *Ibid.*, p. 140.

28. *Ibid.*, p. 154.

29. Clark, I, 314.

30. *Ibid.*, p. 311.

31. *Ibid.*

32. *New France and New England*, pp. 202-3.

33. "University Reform," *Darwinism and Other Essays* (Boston and New York, 1885), p. 289.

34. *Ibid.*, p. 292.

35. *Ibid.*, pp. 330-31.

36. "A Philosophy of Art," *The Unseen World and Other Essays* (Boston, 1876), p. 282.

37. *Ibid.*, p. 284.

38. *Letters*, p. 170.

39. *Ibid.,* p. 180.
40. *Ibid.,* p. 183.
41. *Ibid.,* p. 177.
42. *Ibid.,* p. 172.
43. *Ibid.,* p. 181.
44. *Ibid.,* p. 212.
45. *Ibid.,* p. 200.
46. *Myths and Mythmakers* (Boston, 1900), p. 16.
47. *Ibid.,* p. 21.
48. *Ibid.,* p. 38.
49. *Ibid.,* p. 39.

Chapter Three

1. *Letters,* p. 324.
2. *Ibid.,* p. 263.
3. *Ibid.,* p. 239.
4. *Ibid.,* p. 228.
5. *Ibid.,* p. 238.
6. Clark, I, 529.
7. *Letters,* p. 233.
8. *Ibid.,* p. 266.
9. *Ibid.,* p. 281. An interesting esthetic footnote is an observation from the same letter: "The Raphael pictures are kept in a room by themselves, alone in their glory. They are nothing but simple chalkwork, painted or drawn off-hand, without anything to go by, and I think they show the astonishing power of the artist even more than finished paintings would."
10. *Ibid.,* p. 315.
11. *Ibid.,* p. 327.
12. *Ibid.,* p. 278.
13. *Ibid.,* p. 271.
14. "Evolution and the Present Age," *Essays Historical and Literary,* II, 282.
15. *Outlines of Cosmic Philosophy* (Boston, 1874).
16. *Ibid.,* pp. 39-41. All quotations in this paragraph unless otherwise noted.
17. "Herbert Spencer's Service to Religion," *Essays Historical and Literary,* II, 235.
18. *Cosmic Philosophy,* I, 276.
19. *Ibid.,* II, 183.
20. *Ibid.,* II, 189.
21. *Ibid.,* II, 403.
22. *Ibid.,* II, 342.
23. *Ibid.,* I, 353.

24. *Ibid.*, I, 308.
25. *Ibid.*, I, 416.
26. Clark, II, 55-56.
27. "The Unseen World," *The Unseen World and Other Essays*, pp. 56-57.
28. *Ibid.*, p. 58.
29. *Letters*, p. 374.
30. *The Destiny of Man* (Boston, 1893), p. 107.
31. *Ibid.*, pp. 110-11.
32. *Ibid.*, p. 116.
33. *Ibid.*, pp. 118-19.
34. Clark, II, 322.
35. *The Idea of God* (Boston, 1895), preface, pp. xix-xx.
36. *Ibid.*, p. 50.
37. *Ibid.*, p. 59.
38. *Ibid.*, p. 167.
39. *Harper's Monthly*, LXXII (April, 1886), pp. 808-9.
40. *Through Nature to God* (Boston, 1901), pp. 19-21.
41. *Letters*, p. 87.
42. *Through Nature to God*, pp. 38-39.
43. *Ibid.*, p. 41.
44. *Ibid.*, p. 63.
45. *Ibid.*, pp. 64-65.
46. *Ibid.*, pp. 66-71.
47. *Ibid.*, p. 79.
48. *Ibid.*, p. 129.
49. *Ibid.*, pp. 193-94.
50. *Cosmic Philosophy*, I, 397.

Chapter Four

1. *Letters*, p. 375.
2. *Ibid.*, p. 379.
3. *Ibid.*, p. 368.
4. *Ibid.*, p. 391.
5. Clark, II, 140.
6. "John Tyndall," *Essays Historical and Literary*, II, 246.
7. *Letters*, p. 418.
8. *Ibid.*, p. 421.
9. Clark, II, 192-93.
10. *Ibid.*, II, 198.
11. *Ibid.*, II, 198-99.
12. *Letters*, p. 480.
13. *Ibid.*, p. 519.
14. *Ibid.*, p. 503. Fiske clipped this note and sent it in a letter

with the indication that he approved of the comment.

15. Clark, II, 350.
16. *Letters*, p. 537.
17. *Ibid.*, p. 539.
18. Clark, II, 398.
19. *Ibid.*, II, 405-6.
20. *Through Nature to God*, p. 177.
21. *Letters*, p. 604.
22. "Old and New Ways of Treating History," *Essays Historical and Literary*, II, p. 20.

Chapter Five

1. "Old and New Ways of Treating History," p. 23.
2. *Cosmic Philosophy*, I, 166.
3. *American Political Ideas* (New York, 1901), p. 6.
4. *The Critical Period in American History* (Boston, 1888), p. 357.
5. *The Beginnings of New England* (Boston, 1896), pp. 32-33.
6. *Ibid.*, p. 145.
7. *Ibid.*, pp. 57-58.
8. *Ibid.*, p. 14.
9. *Ibid.*, p. 24.
10. Clark, II, 396.
11. *The Discovery of America* (Boston, 1892), I, 45.
12. *Ibid.*, I, 255.
13. *Ibid.*, I, 102-3.
14. *Ibid.*, I, 169.
15. *Old Virginia and Her Neighbors* (Boston, 1897), I, 18-19.
16. *Ibid.*, I, 37.
17. *Ibid.*, p. 64.
18. *Ibid.*, I, 228.
19. Mrs. Schuyler Van Rensellaer, "Mr. Fiske and the History of New York," *North American Review*, CLXXIII, 87 (August, 1901), 171-72.
20. *The Dutch and Quaker Colonies* (Boston, 1899), I, 30.
21. *Ibid.*, I, 130-31.
22. "Old and New Ways of Treating History," *Essays*, II, 20.
23. *Dutch and Quaker Colonies*, II, 355-56.
24. Mrs. Van Rensellaer, pp. 172-73.
25. *Ibid.*, p. 187.
26. The personal reasons were, of course, based on his early clash with the Reverend Taylor. Scientific reasons are summarized in the rest of the paragraph.
27. *Dutch and Quaker Colonies*, II, 105-7.
28. *Ibid.*, II, 308.

29. *Ibid.*, II, 354-55.

30. "Thomas Jefferson, the Conservative Reformer," *Essays*, II, 163. For confirmation that Fiske was not happy with the Spanish-American War, see Berman, pp. 251-52.

Chapter Six

1. Clark, II, 409-10.

2. James Brooks, "Address," *One Hundred and Fiftieth Anniversary*, Petersham, Massachusetts (August 10, 1904), Historical Society, pp. 42-43.

3. Elbert Hubbard, "John Fiske," *Little Journeys to the Homes of Great Scientists*, XVII (December, 1905), p. 146.

4. "Giants of Yesterday," Boston *Transcript* (Saturday, June 11, 1911).

5. Horton and Edwards, *Backgrounds of American Literary Thought* (New York, 1952), pp. 157-58.

6. "Athenian and American Life," *The Unseen World*, p. 335.

7. Richard Eastman, *A Guide to the Novel* (San Francisco, 1965), p. 124.

8. Quoted by Henry Steele Commager, *The American Mind* (New Haven, 1950), p. 114.

9. *Ibid.*, p. 115.

10. *Ibid.*, p. 128.

11. Theodore Parker materials are collected in Perry Miller, *The Transcendentalists* (Cambridge, 1950), p. 321.

12. *Ibid.*, p. 416. Taken from "The Writings of Ralph Waldo Emerson," *The Massachusetts Quarterly*, III (March, 1850), pp. 200-255.

13. Clark, II, 497.

14. *Ibid.*, II, 480.

15. *Ibid.*, II, 482.

16. "Evolution and the Present Age," *Essays*, II, 276.

17. "John Milton," *Essays*, II, 40.

18. "Daniel Webster and the Sentiment of Union," *Essays*, I, 389.

19. *Ibid.*, p. 381.

20. *Cosmic Philosophy*, II, 85.

21. *Ibid.*, I, 237.

22. "Nathan the Wise," *The Unseen World*, pp. 165-67.

23. Allen Tate, *Collected Essays* (Chicago, 1959), cited in John J. Encke, *Academic Discourse* (New York, 1964), p. 167.

24. "Connecticut's Influence on the Federal Constitution," *Essays*, II, 126.

25. *Ibid.*

26. "The Story of a New England Town," p. 722.

27. "Old and New Ways of Treating History," *Essays,* II, 6.

28. "The Deeper Significance of the Boston Tea Party," *Essays,* II, 165.

29. Clark, I, 302.

30. "Spain and the Netherlands," *The Unseen World,* p. 224.

31. Clark, I, 302.

32. Winsor and Fiske, "Francis Parkman," *Atlantic Monthly,* LXXIII (May, 1894), p. 674.

33. Clark, II, 72.

34. Winsor, "Francis Parkman," p. 662.

35. *Ibid.,* p. 663.

36. *Ibid.*

37. Fiske, "Francis Parkman," p. 665.

38. *Ibid.,* p. 667.

39. Francis Parkman, *North American Review,* LXXIV (January, 1852), 150-52.

40. Commager, *The American Mind,* p. 296.

41. "Andrew Jackson, Frontiersman and Soldier," *Essays,* I, 224.

42. Vernon L. Parrington, *Main Currents in American Thought* (New York, 1930), III, 211.

43. See works cited above by Parrington, Commager, and Berman. Also Richard Hofstadter, *Social Darwinism in American Thought* (Philadelphia, 1945); Van Wyck Brooks, *New England: Indian Summer* (New York, 1940).

Selected Bibliography

PRIMARY SOURCES

The most complete, though not definitive, edition of Fiske's works is *The Writings of John Fiske* (Cambridge: Houghton Mifflin, 1902). The most complete bibliographies are in Berman, *John Fiske* (Cambridge: Harvard University Press, 1961) and Spiller et al., *Literary History of the United States,* vol. III (New York: The Macmillan Co., 1948). Various collections of letters are available, most notable being the manuscript collection in the Henry L. Huntington Library. The task of collecting all of Fiske's shorter writings has yet to be performed. The following titles, arranged chronologically, are those referred to in the present study.

Tobacco and Alcohol. New York: Leypoldt and Holt, 1869.
Myths and Mythmakers. New York: Osgood, 1873.
Outlines of Cosmic Philosophy. Boston: Houghton Mifflin, 1874.
The Unseen World and Other Essays. Boston: Houghton Mifflin, 1876.
Darwinism and Other Essays. Boston: Houghton Mifflin, 1879.
The Destiny of Man. Boston: Houghton Mifflin, 1884.
The Idea of God. Boston: Houghton Mifflin, 1885.
American Political Ideas. New York: Harper and Brothers, 1885.
The Critical Period of American History. Boston: Houghton Mifflin, 1888.
The Beginnings of New England. Boston: Houghton Mifflin, 1889.
The Discovery of America. Boston: Houghton Mifflin, 1892.
Old Virginia and Her Neighbors. Boston: Houghton Mifflin, 1897.
The Dutch and Quaker Colonies in America. Boston: Houghton Mifflin, 1899.
Through Nature to God. Boston: Houghton Mifflin, 1899.
New France and New England. Boston: Houghton Mifflin, 1902.
Essays Historical and Literary. New York: The Macmillan Co., 1902.

SECONDARY SOURCES

ADAMS, BROOKS. *The Law of Civilization and Decay.* New York: Vintage Books, 1955. Most useful for comparative treatment of theories on "laws of history." In the preface to *The Beginnings of New England,* Fiske cites Brooks Adams as a "former pupil."

169

ADAMS, HENRY. *History of the United States during the First Administration of Thomas Jefferson.* New York: Charles Scribner's Sons, 1889. Reissue of the first six chapters of volume one under the title *The United States in 1800.* Ithaca: Cornell University Press, 1962. Invaluable for perspectives on Fiske as a historian.

BERMAN, MILTON. *John Fiske.* Cambridge: Harvard University Press, 1961. Only modern scholarly biography of Fiske. A most perceptive study; focus on careful definition of Fiske as popularizer.

BOWEN, CATHERINE DRINKER. *Yankee from Olympus.* Boston: Little, Brown and Company, 1944. Provides valuable information about Harvard during the middle and late nineteenth century.

BROOKS, JAMES. "Address." *One Hundred and Fiftieth Anniversary, Petersham.* Petersham, Massachusetts. n.p., 1904. Includes a memorial to Fiske by his brother-in-law; also a poem on Petersham by Fiske's son Ralph.

CLARK, JOHN SPENCER. *John Fiske, The Life and Letters.* Boston and New York: Houghton Mifflin, 1917. Most dependable biography by a friend. Leans strongly on letters; contains no notes or bibliography.

FISK, ETHEL. *The Letters of John Fiske.* New York: The Macmillan Co., 1940. Unfortunately, Fiske's daughter is a most unscholarly editor. By cross-checking with Clark, it is reasonably safe to make judicious use of her collection. The Fiske student concerned with accuracy is directed to manuscript collections, especially those in the Henry L. Huntington Library and Art Gallery, San Francisco.

FISKE, JOHN. *Two Hundredth Anniversary Celebration.* Petersham, Massachusetts. n.p., 1954. Contains an address by Fiske's grandson and a pleasant summary of the town which was Fiske's beloved summer home.

HOSMER, JAMES K. "Giants of Yesterday," Boston *Transcript.* Saturday, June 11, 1911. Personal reminiscences of Bancroft, Prescott, and Fiske by a friend and colleague.

HOUGHTON, WALTER E. *The Victorian Frame of Mind.* New Haven: Yale University Press, 1957. Invaluable reference for gaining a balanced perspective on the period.

VAN RENSELLAER, MRS. SCHUYLER. "Mr. Fiske and the History of New York," *North American Review,* vol. CLXXIII, no. 87 (August, 1901). Useful review to illustrate contemporary criticism of Fiske as a historian.

Index

(The works of John Fiske are listed under his name)

171

172